BECOMING A SHEPHERD

BECOMING A SHEPHERD

Contemporary Pastoral Ministry

Oliver McMahan

CLEVELAND, TENNESSEE 37311

Library of Congress Catalog Card Number: 94-068386

ISBN: 0871481162

Copyright © 1994 by Pathway Press

Cleveland, Tennessee 37311

To my wife,
Martha,
with love

Contents

Contents

Foreword

In this day of advertising buzzwords, media sound bites, and high-tech phrases—in this time of uncertain theological interpretations, strange theories of Scripture, and confused meanings of ministry—there is an urgent need for a practical, down-to-earth, scripturally sensitive look at the Word in action for relevant church leadership in a secularized society.

In this book, *Becoming a Shepherd*, Oliver McMahan achieves this goal by accurately defining biblical terms and succinctly carving out an expositional understanding of the scriptural context for effective Kingdom life in tempestuous times.

Drawing from his rich background of experience as a pastor, teacher, and church planter, Dr. McMahan charts the meaning behind the message with clarity and conviction.

Having known Oliver from his childhood and having had the pleasure of ministering with him in church and pastors conferences, I can recommend this book as one born out of a life dedicated to the principles presented.

Becoming a Shepherd is one of those foundational texts to be referred to again and again by pastors, church leaders, and laypersons in every phase of church ministry. It is a reliable resource for clarifying and communicating the revelation of God through the church to the world.

As author McMahan states, "The goal of the church is not merely to reform men on earth but to see their souls won for eternity."

Paul L. Walker, Ph.D.
Senior Pastor
Mount Paran Church of God
Atlanta, Georgia

Preface

Various methods can be used to describe shepherding. The example of contemporary pastors is a source of valuable information and insight, as well as the perspective of pastors down through the centuries since the inception of the church. Another important source of instruction is data collected from a large number of pastors; however, the primary method used in this volume is the commentary of the Scripture texts that apply to the ministry of shepherding. Studies of these texts and their emphases are presented, and applications are made based on conclusions drawn from these texts.

Through the years clergymen have tried various methods and trends of pastoring. Some of these trends have become popular for a time and then passed with the introduction of more effective and relevant methods. However, certain fundamental principles presented in Scripture are not subject to such change. These principles form the focus of this work.

The reader can use the scriptural insights provided in this volume for contemporary ministry. The studies and texts given here offer pastors the opportunity to consider recent methods in light of scriptural principles. Further, as new methods are introduced, these texts can be used to assess their scriptural soundness.

The Bible presents the shepherding of God's people seriously. Shepherding is a vital function which God instituted for the care of His flock. Messages of instruction, judgment, and exhortation call both shepherd and flock to faithfulness. Therefore, it is our duty to respond biblically.

Acknowledgments

The scriptural insights discussed in this volume reflect ministry principles and methods that have been used in a number of pastoral settings. Having served as pastor, associate senior pastor, and staff member in various settings, I gratefully acknowledge the privilege of ministering together with these congregations—Traver Church of God, Traver, California; Oak Cliff Church of God (currently Mount View Church of God), Dallas, Texas; Total Life Center Church of God, Minot, North Dakota; and Mount Olive Church of God, Cleveland, Tennessee.

These concepts from Scripture have especially formed much of the ministry with the Mount Olive Church, where I serve as associate senior pastor. I give heartfelt thanks to senior pastor Gary Sears and the Mount Olive staff and family. Senior pastor Sears has led us in perceiving the answer to the question "What is God doing in your church?" Under his leadership the church has organized itself around that answer, fulfilling the mandate to be a God-centered church.

A special note of gratitude is due my wife, Martha; my son, Jonathan; and my daughter, Holly. Their love and cominstry in the harvest are assets in the work to which God has called me.

Introduction

The elders which are among you I exhort, who am also an elder, and a witness of the sufferings of Christ, and also a partaker of the glory that shall be revealed: Feed the flock of God which is among you, taking the oversight thereof, not by constraint, but willingly; not for filthy lucre, but of a ready mind; neither as being lords over God's heritage, but being ensamples to the flock. And when the chief Shepherd shall appear, ye shall receive a crown of glory that fadeth not away. Likewise, ye younger, submit yourselves unto the elder. Yea, all of you be subject one to another, and be clothed with humility: for God resisteth the proud, and giveth grace to the humble. Humble yourselves therefore under the mighty hand of God, that he may exalt you in due time: casting all your care upon him; for he careth for you. Be sober, be vigilant; because your adversary the devil, as a roaring lion, walketh about, seeking whom he may devour (1 Peter 5:1-8).

The Mandate to Nourish the Body of Christ

The "job description" of pastoral leadership is found in 1 Peter 5:1-8. This description is twofold, namely, to feed and to have oversight.

The word *feed* indicates the function of providing nourishment and sustenance for the flock. The people of God need the spiritual food that comes from a rich diet of prayer and the Word. The pastor has the responsibility to lead the flock of the Lord to pastures where they can feed spiritually. Then the Holy Spirit quickens the prayer life and the ministry of the Word in the believer.

The word *feed* in verse 2 is from the Greek term *poimaino*, which means "to tend as a shepherd." In effect, then, this exhortation is to "shepherd the flock of God." This indicates the closeness of the concept of nourishing with shepherding.

The Mandate to Provide Protective Oversight

The second part of Peter's "job description" is to provide protective oversight. The word *oversight* is translated from the Greek word *episkopeo*, which means "to oversee." It indicates the watchful care one exercises over another.

One of the major tasks of the shepherd is protecting the flock. The greatest danger sheep face is the peril of wild animals. The plight of the unprotected flock is much more prominent in Scripture than the danger of an undernourished flock. If a shepherd neglects the flock, they will not starve, according to scriptural illustrations. The more immediate danger is lack of protection.

In the major biblical descriptions of sheep without a shepherd, the picture is of sheep that have been slaughtered because the shepherd failed to give them proper protection. An example of this depiction is found in Matthew 9:36: "But when he saw the multitudes, he was moved with compassion on them, because they fainted, and were scattered abroad [also slaughtered], as sheep having no shepherd." Thus, the shepherd has the responsibility of protecting the flock from danger.

The Character of the Shepherd

The largest portion of Peter's address deals with the shepherd's character, from which flows his devotion and courage. These qualities, along with his personal stamina and moral character, give the shepherd his ability to perform his many duties. This is Peter's emphasis in verses 2b-3.

Constraint indicates someone who works only because he is forced to or manipulated into doing so. This refers to someone who does not have the inner motivation and calling to minister. His response is not godly obedience but doing a job motivated only by pressure or necessity.

Willingly is similar to the eager volunteer spirit required by God when He spoke of a willing heart in Exodus 35. This was a major requirement for those deemed worthy to construct the tabernacle. In the same sense, God requires that pastors have an inner motivation fed by devotion to Him.

Filthy lucre comes from a Greek term meaning "shameful gain." It implies the accomplishment of a task for the wrong motive. A focus merely upon outcome with no consideration of the appropriateness or godliness of the motive leads to it. Peter was concerned that the shepherd have a strong sense of purpose and godly motivation.

Ready mind expresses the energy that comes from proper motivation. A certain peace and resourcefulness come from godly devotion. Ministry does not thrive merely on the outcome. Rather, it is the eagerness of the soul that is the shepherd's lasting resource.

Lords over God's heritage is not just a haughty and condescending attitude. Peter was emphasizing rather that leaders must not try to assume the authority over something that is not actually theirs. This does not preclude the appropriate exercise of leadership. Assertiveness in leadership is not only allowed but expected when situations call for decisive action. Peter was speaking against the presumptive thought that the final authority is in the hands of the shepherd. All pastoral action must be submitted to the lordship of Christ. This is the perspective of authority which Peter advocated.

Ensamples (examples) does not mean merely the rigor of physical activity. This is more than just the example of hard work. The meaning of the word is made clear by the phrase that precedes it regarding lordship. The shepherd must be an example in following the lordship of Christ. The shepherd does not assume final authority for the flock but exhibits instead a profound recognition of the leadership of Christ over all His sheep. This theme is continued in verse 4.

The Mandate of Christ's Shepherding

Peter climaxed his appeal to human shepherds by pointing to the One who shepherds both the flock *and* the shepherds. Peter finished the section on character by emphasizing the proper use of authority. The lordship of the Chief Shepherd was Peter's final emphasis in this passage. It is to be the goal and the source of authority of those who shepherd the body of Christ.

The Eternal Dimension of the Mandate

In the context of Christ as the Chief Shepherd, Peter declared the eternal dimension of shepherding that is possible because of Christ. The Chief Shepherd enables the shepherds of the church to see their work supersede the bounds of human achievement and result. The goal of the church is not merely to reform men on earth but to see their souls won for eternity.

This eternal perspective is necessary for proper pastoral function. The crown of glory is a recognition of the accomplishment of Christ through the shepherd. The godly ministry of shepherding is not only worthy, it is also eternal.

1

BIBLICAL THEMES ON THE ON THE PASTOR-SHEPHERD

Old Testament Themes for the Shepherd

1

The term *shepherd* can refer to an individual who helps others, or it might indicate someone who keeps others nourished. A shepherd can also be a person who shows loving care and concern. Two primary functions in Scripture describe the work of a shepherd: to nourish and to protect the flock. This chapter will look at these two important concepts.

In the ancient Hebrew text, the word *shepherd* is not rooted in identity with the sheep but is from a term identified with feeding. The word for shepherd is *ra'ah*. It derived from the word for *feed*. As a result, the shepherd was known as "the one who feeds."

The Principles and Applications of Ezekiel 34:1-22

Woe Upon Shepherds Who Feed Themselves (Ezekiel 34:1-3)

Son of man, prophesy against the shepherds of Israel,

prophesy, and say unto them, Thus saith the Lord God
unto the shepherds; Woe be to the shepherds of Israel
that do feed themselves! should not the shepherds feed
the flocks? (34:2).

The message of Ezekiel 34 is a primary statement of the
Old Testament perspective of pastoring. Those who had
led the nation of Judah had a pastoral function. This
included rulers as well as religious leaders. Both had a
responsibility for the care of the nation. The emphasis is
on the spiritual care of the people.

In verse 2 a woe and indictment is spoken against the
shepherds. The pastors of the nation were guilty of one
glaring sin, feeding themselves instead of feeding the
sheep. This is the opposite of the description given in John
10:11 of the Good Shepherd, who gives His life for the
sheep. The latter part of Ezekiel 34:2 asks whether the
shepherds should have been feeding the flock as opposed
to selfishly feeding themselves.

The application of this indictment is challenging. If a
pastor is not earnestly endeavoring to feed the flock, he
may have succumbed to the temptation to feed only himself. The serious indictment that follows is indicative of
the attitude of God toward this particular sin. Although the
contemporary pastor has an obligation to cultivate his own
spiritual relationship with God, this does not relinquish
him from his God-called obligation to nurture the flock.
God's stinging accusation of those guilty of such a practice
is clear: "Ye eat the fat, and ye clothe you with the wool,
ye kill them that are fed: but ye feed not the flock" (34:3).

In this verse God lists the ways in which the pastors had
been feeding themselves. They had reserved the best for
themselves. They had been concerned only with protecting
themselves. As a result, they had killed the flock. The

description builds in intensity with each element. The final indictment was a chilling picture of what happens when pastors become selfish and neglect the sheep.

First, they reserved for themselves the best of the resources. These had been intended for the sheep, but the shepherds used them for themselves. *Fat* in the ancient world represented the best part of the animal. It was a delicacy and a source of special nourishment.

Second, the shepherds removed the wool that protected the sheep and used it to protect themselves. Though the sheep were regularly sheared of their wool, the indication in this verse is that the wool was removed at the wrong time and in the wrong manner.

Third, the pastors had taken the life of the sheep. Without necessary resources for nourishment and no protective covering, the sheep were subject to malnourishment and slaughter. And God held the shepherds accountable.

At times, sheep may be rebellious and wander from the care of the pastor. In those cases, the sheep bear the responsibility. However, pastors who feed only themselves and neglect the flock are held accountable for the death of the sheep.

How the Shepherds Neglected the Flock
(Ezekiel 34:4-6)

> The diseased have ye not strengthened, neither have ye healed that which was sick, neither have ye bound up that which was broken, neither have ye brought again that which was driven away, neither have ye sought that which was lost; but with force and with cruelty have ye ruled them (34:4).

This verse gives an amplified description of the three

major elements of verse 3. This description with its specific parts can be analyzed as follows:

Scripture	Pastoral Function That Should Have Been Done
"The diseased have ye not strengthened"	Relief of pain
"healed that which was sick"	Ministry of healing
"bound up that which was broken"	Repairing the dysfunctional
"brought again that which was driven away"	Restoration and reconciliation
"sought that which was lost"	Evangelism
"with force and with cruelty have ye ruled them"	Ministerial compassion

God outlined in verse 4 the specific areas of pastoral function that had been neglected by these shepherds. These areas were essential to the work that needed to have been done by them. Their failure was not just a personal one, but their work was affected as well. The tragedy of personal overindulgence by these shepherds was at the same time a crisis of neglected responsibility toward the sheep. "And they were scattered, because there is no shepherd: and they became meat to all the beasts of the field, when they were scattered" (34:5).

The result of the neglect of the shepherds was the scattering and slaughter of the sheep. Scattered not only indicated the wandering of the sheep, but it also indicated that the sheep were driven in various directions. They ran in fear and desperation because there was no leadership or care. They were left without protection. The immediate danger was not malnourishment but slaughter. "My sheep wandered through all the mountains, and upon every high hill: yea, my flock was scattered upon all the face of the earth, and none did search or seek after them" (34:6)

This verse repeats much of what was stated earlier. The one difference is that God identified the sheep as His own. They had always been and would continue to be His. The pastors whom God had accused of feeding only themselves had not been commissioned merely to guard and feed a group of people, but they had been given the responsibility of watching God's own possession. The personal pronoun *my* occurs twice in this passage. God said it was His sheep who wandered and His flock that was scattered. Pastoral neglect is vividly portrayed by the phrase "none did search or seek after them."

The implications of not fulfilling the calling and function of a pastor is not just sociological and limited to the human dynamics of individual members of a flock; the impact is eternal. The dimensions of such a tragedy reach into the heavens to God himself. God is personally affected by the perils a congregation faces, because the church is ultimately His personal possession. A pastor must remind himself of the eternal dimension of this divine truth.

The Pastor-Shepherds Who Neglected the Flock of the Lord (Ezekiel 34:7-10a)

Therefore, ye shepherds, hear the word of the Lord; As I

live, saith the Lord God, surely because my flock
became a prey, and my flock became meat to every
beast of the field, because there was no shepherd, neither did my shepherds search for my flock, but the shepherds fed themselves, and fed not my flock; therefore, O
ye shepherds, hear the word of the Lord; Thus saith the
Lord God; Behold, I am against the shepherds; and I
will require my flock at their hand, and cause them to
cease from feeding the flock; neither shall the shepherds
feed themselves any more (34:7-10a).

In this section God summarized the woes He placed
against the shepherds who fed themselves at the expense of
the flock. There are four primary emphases. The first
emphasis is God's relationship to these pastors: He was
"against" them. He was no longer their sustainer and
guide. He was now their adversary.

The second emphasis is God's requirement of accountability for these pastor's selfishness. God holds pastors
directly responsible for the consequences of their own mis-
deeds. The pastor is not blamed for the irresponsibility of
individual members of the flock. God holds those members who are rebellious and wicked responsible for their
own actions. Nevertheless, God makes it clear that the
pastor is personally accountable for the care of the flock.

The third emphasis is God's termination of those shepherd's function with that flock. God personally caused
"them to cease from feeding the flock." The emphasis is
not upon the manner in which God did this but rather that
the damage being done to the flock was stopped.

The final emphasis is God's removal of the shepherd's
ability to feed himself at the expense of the sheep. The
result of the action of removing the shepherd was twofold:
a punishment against the shepherd and a benefit to the

sheep. It highlighted God's loving concern for them and set the stage for the personal intervention of God that followed.

God's Personal Intervention for the Neglected Flock (Ezekiel 34:10b)

> For I will deliver my flock from their mouth, that they may not be meat for them (34:10).

God made a powerful declaration. The flock belonged to Him. The shepherds may have assumed the flock was their possession to treat as they pleased. Now, especially when the flock had been misused, God clarified who owned the sheep. They were His own special possession.

The metaphor of this short section is powerful. The sheep are pictured as being in the mouth of the shepherd. The revelation is that the shepherds were not only feeding themselves *instead* of the sheep, but they were also feeding *on* the sheep. This is the tragic outcome of neglect in pastoral ministry. When a shepherd is overly concerned with his own needs to the neglect and abuse of the flock, he begins consciously or unconsciously to take advantage of them.

The Work of God to Do What Human Shepherds Neglected to Do (Ezekiel 34:11-16)

> For thus saith the Lord God; Behold, I, even I, will both search my sheep, and seek them out. As a shepherd seeketh out his flock in the day that he is among his sheep that are scattered; so will I seek out my sheep (34:11, 12a).

God powerfully emphasized His personal intervention for the sheep. The words "Behold, I, even I" represent a statement amplified three times. *Behold* called attention to God's pivotal work. The time had now come for decisive intervention. The sheep were already in the mouths of the self-seeking shepherds, and God was now intervening. The two "I" statements stress that God himself personally intervened. There was no other resource for rescue. Those whom God had ordained to care for His sheep had failed to do so.

This entire passage is both a call for responsible pastoral ministry and a comfort to any congregation. God promised here that He will hold pastors accountable for their neglect to fulfill their pastoral duties. Even their privilege to function in pastoral ministry could be removed by intervention from God. The particular method of removal may vary, but the result will be God's intervention nevertheless.

This section of Scripture also assures the congregation that God will intervene by searching and seeking for those who may have been hurt or driven away. *Search* indicates that God's goal is to reconcile the individuals in the church unto Himself. The intensity and fervor by which He does this is conveyed by the use of the word *seek*. He will continually look for them no matter where they may be and no matter what their condition. God's love for His people is unfathomable and unquenchable. He is constantly intervening for them and seeking them out to minister to them. They may have rebelled because of inconsistencies in leadership; nevertheless, the message of this verse is that God is still willing to "seek them out."

> [I] will deliver them out of all places where they have been scattered in the cloudy and dark day. And I will bring them out from the people, and gather them from the countries, and will bring them to their own land, and

feed them upon the mountains of Israel by the rivers, and in all the inhabited places of the country. I will feed them in a good pasture, and upon the high mountains of Israel shall their fold be: there shall they lie in a good fold, and in a fat pasture shall they feed upon the mountains of Israel. I will feed my flock, and I will cause them to lie down, saith the Lord God (34:12b-15).

This section describes God as the shepherd of His people, who protects, feeds, and delivers them from danger. The Hebrew word translated "deliver" pictures a decisive, almost explosive action, in which someone is pulled or plucked out of the very jaws or grasp of an adversary. The fuller nature of the deliverance is pictured in the series of phrases, "bring them out," "gather thee," "feed thee," and "good pasture." These terms describe a process by which God not only delivers but also nurtures. The convert must receive "good pasture" and feed on the things of the Lord once deliverance and salvation have taken place. Sheep require times of rest to digest their food. These times are parallel to the necessity of meditating on and gleaning from the Word and fellowship. The wise shepherd provides times for those in the church to incorporate the Word more fully into their lives.

I will seek that which was lost, and bring again that which was driven away, and will bind up that which was broken, and will strengthen that which was sick: but I will destroy the fat and the strong; I will feed them with judgment (34:16).

This verse lists five final aspects of God's work as shepherd of His people. These, as do the previous five aspects in verses 11-15, provide a paradigm for pastoral work today. The pastor must be evangelistic. He may not be specifically called to be an evangelist; however, his work must include seeking the lost. Seeking implies "searching diligently with the desire to obtain." This means the pastor's concern for the lost should not be satisfied until the sinner is brought to salvation. This persistence is the kind of seeking God does in behalf of His people.

The pastor must also be involved in the ministry of reconciliation. This is the force of the phrase "bring again that which was driven away." Regardless of the reason, the individual is in peril as long as he is outside the protection of the fold. The context of the phrase implies that the person may have been "driven away" because of dangers from within as well as outside of the flock. Nevertheless, the call of the pastor is to go out and bring that individual back. This is further work of God himself as shepherd.

The ministry of pastoring also includes healing and nourishment. The sheep are pictured here as broken and sick. Every component of the pastor's ministry can have a therapeutic dimension. The brokenness of lives will persist without intervention. God works for the healing of the individual, and the pastor must work to facilitate and usher in God's work. Nourishment is a necessary complement to healing. Without it, full recovery is not possible. These complementary works are part of the paradigm of God's example of a shepherd.

The final work described is discernment. The term *judgment* does not imply the eternal condition of the soul. Rather, the term indicates the work of ordering and directing the church for greater effectiveness and the benefit of those within. The sheep left to themselves would crowd some out and trample others. Discretion and administration is required to guide the flock so that all are nourished and protected.

God's Judgment Through His Work of Discernment (Ezekiel 34:17-22)

> And as for you, O my flock, thus saith the Lord God; Behold, I judge between cattle and cattle, between the rams and the he goats. Seemeth it a small thing unto you to have eaten up the good pasture, but ye must tread down with your feet the residue of your pastures? and to have drunk of the deep waters, but ye must foul the residue with your feet? And as for my flock, they eat that which ye have trodden with your feet; and they drink that which ye have fouled with your feet. Therefore thus saith the Lord God unto them; Behold, I, even I, will judge between the fat cattle and between the lean cattle. Because ye have thrust with side and with shoulder, and pushed all the diseased with your horns, till ye have scattered them abroad; therefore will I save my flock, and they shall no more be a prey; and I will judge between cattle and cattle (34:17-22).

This section highlights an often-neglected aspect of pastoral work, judgment and discretion. God sets forth a pattern for those in pastoral ministry today to follow. God's purpose is to protect the sheep from one another, to keep the sheep from destroying the pastures which nourish them, and to shield the sheep from outside dangers. This passage is realistic enough to identify the perils within the flock as well as those from the outside. The indictment is that without this function, the people of a church not only can starve spiritually and be attacked from outside dangers, but they can also destroy one another. Yet this function of pastoral ministry is often neglected.

The image painted by these verses is of the flock crowding one another out, even gouging one another with their horns. Cattle and goats are mentioned with sheep because the ancient shepherd frequently had larger animals to watch over along with the sheep. The modern-day pastor must discern the needs of each member and watchfully provide an edifying context for every individual. This may even prompt warnings, admonitions, or rebukes that guard against individuals taking advantage of one another in a church.

These verses also look toward the condition of the pasture when the flock is left to abusive practices. It has been selfishly stripped and the waters have been muddied and undrinkable. This can occur in a church. Because of spiritual immaturity and selfish indulgence, some people in a congregation may consume the resources of the church. As a result, others are left unfed. The muddied waters refer to impurities in doctrine. Because of a lack of spiritual depth, pride and compromise allow the purity of the doctrine of the church to be tainted. These abuses call for the discerning, judging function of the pastor.

The resounding promise in the latter part of this passage is that God himself assures the protection and judgment of the flock. Church members can petition God directly and receive from Him when there is a failure on the part of the shepherd. This guarantee is important in light of the reality of ministerial failure.

New Testament Themes for the Shepherd

2

And I will set up one shepherd over them, and he shall feed them, even my servant David; he shall feed them, and he shall be their shepherd. And I the Lord will be their God, and my servant David a prince among them; I the Lord have spoken it (Ezekiel 34:23, 24).

In these verses God said He will supply another shepherd. This is a prophetic section, referring to events to come in God's end-time plan for Israel. There have been various interpretations of the exact fulfillment of this prophecy. Three interpretations of who "David" refers to have included the Messiah, David himself, or an end-time ruler over Israel in the Millennium. The specific end-time fulfillment of the prophecy remains to be seen.

Nevertheless, the principle of God's provision of a shepherd for His people remains firm. The fulfillment of this verse has implications for the shepherd-pastor ministry found in the New Testament. Christ is the Great Shepherd of the church; however, He also uses human shepherds. The idea that God provides shepherds for the churches is foundational for understanding the importance of the shepherd's office and function in the New Testament.

Ultimately the message of this chapter is that God is the shepherd of His people. Even though human shepherds may fail, God is the final shepherd of His people. The ministry of the church and its shepherds should be built upon God's own work in their midst. This is the concluding message of this great chapter:

> Thus shall they know that I the Lord their God am with them, and that they, even the house of Israel, are my people, saith the Lord God. And ye my flock, the flock of my pasture, are men, and I am your God, saith the Lord God (Ezekiel 34:30, 31).

The recognition of God's sovereign ability to supply for His people is the primary message of this chapter. The neglect of the shepherds that had been feeding and protecting the people was great; in fact, the flock had become open prey. Nevertheless, God intervened so that His people might know He is still God.

The greatest calamity that can befall a church is to forget that God is God. Without the recognition of God's deity and almighty ability to intervene in behalf of His people, a congregation will become vulnerable and open prey to heresy and destruction. The loss of praise, adoration, and discernment of His sovereign care only perpetuates the spiritual malnourishment and poverty a church may already be experiencing. The greatest peril is to suddenly become a congregation where the presence of God cannot be felt.

Feeding and Shepherding in the New Testament

In the New Testament world, shepherding was looked

down upon. It was considered demeaning and was generally despised. However, the New Testament church held a lofty and godly view of shepherding, using the perspective of the Old Testament.

The Old Testament perspective highlighted the overall task of the shepherd, particularly the twofold function of protecting and feeding. The New Testament also emphasizes this dual responsibility of the shepherd.

Descriptions of the Shepherd, Especially As Fulfilled in Christ

Many of the descriptions of the shepherd in the New Testament are centered on Christ, and these give us insight into the function and definition of a shepherd. Christ saw the multitudes and had compassion on them because they appeared as sheep without a shepherd—directionless, uncared-for, and in distress (Matthew 9:36; Mark 6:34). Christ will act as a shepherd dividing his sheep from the goats at the Judgment (Matthew 25:31-46). Christ is seen as the smitten shepherd on the cross (Matthew 26:31; Mark 14:27). Christ is described as the resurrected shepherd in Hebrews 13:20. Pastors are seen as gifts of grace to the church (Ephesians 4:11).

Descriptions of the Flock

The term *flock, poimnion,* is derived from the same Greek root as the word shepherd, *poimaino.* The flock is described as the ones under the care of the shepherd. This places a vital connection between the sheep and the shepherd—a connection even stronger than the need for pasture or nourishment. The flock of the Lord is destined for per-

secution (Matthew 26:31). They are cared for by the Good
Shepherd (John 10:16). The flock is cared for by a shepherd that in turn receives proper reward (1 Corinthians
9:7). The sheep can safely put their trust in God for their
eternal needs (Luke 12:32). The flock has been purchased
by the blood of Christ, and the shepherd of the flock is
commissioned by the Holy Spirit to feed the flock (Acts
20:28; see also 1 Peter 5:2). They are in danger of attack
from wolves (Acts 20:29). Finally, the flock is to be led by
the example of the shepherd (1 Peter 5:3).

Christ as the Foundation of New Testament Shepherding: Principles of Shepherding As Found in John 10:1-29

The True Shepherd (John 10:1-6)

Verily, verily, I say unto you, He that entereth not by the
door into the sheepfold, but climbeth up some other
way, the same is a thief and a robber (10:1).

Thus Jesus began to describe the care of the true shepherd. Jesus' discourse in chapter 10 is a fitting follow-up
of the narrative in chapter 9 of the healing of the blind
man. Now that the blind man had been healed and had
declared his belief in Jesus, he was in need of a shepherd.

The opening theme of Jesus' description of the shepherd
explains the necessity of protecting the sheep. The sheep
are threatened first of all by those who would attempt to
lead them. This is a much greater threat than any external
peril or lack of food, because the sheep depend on the
shepherd to protect them, to lead them in the right paths,
and to provide proper nourishment. This is why Jesus
emphasized the true shepherd as opposed to one who has

ulterior or selfish motives. The terms *thief* and *robber*
imply not only dishonesty but violence to the sheep. This
is similar to the description in Ezekiel 34. The neglect and
ungodliness of the shepherd put the sheep in peril.

"But he that entereth in by the door is the shepherd of
the sheep. To him the porter openeth" (10:2, 3). The true
shepherd has access to the sheep through the proper entry.
This entry is monitored by the porter. In ancient times, the
sheepfold was usually formed by a stone wall. The sheep
rested within. A number of shepherds may have kept their
sheep together in one fold. When a shepherd wanted his
sheep, he gained access to them through the permission of
the porter.

In the same manner the heavenly Father permits the
entry and access of Christ, the Chief Shepherd, to His own.
Shepherds who abuse their sheep may be tolerated for a
time, but eventually they will be cut off from access to the
congregation and ministry.

"And the sheep hear his voice: and he calleth his own
sheep by name, and leadeth them out. And when he put-
teth forth his own sheep, he goeth before them, and the
sheep follow him: for they know his voice. And a
stranger will they not follow, but will flee from him: for
they know not the voice of strangers" (10:3-5).

In ancient times, once a shepherd had been allowed
access to the sheepfold, he would call for his sheep. The
sheep would respond because they knew not only the commands but also the tone of the shepherd's voice. They
were able to perceive and respond to the voice of their
shepherd. Jesus emphasized the importance of spiritual
perception. In John 9 it was symbolized by sight. In chapter 10 Jesus compared it to recognition of the shepherd's
voice.

The term *know* came from the Greek term *oida,* which means "to perceive and identify." The sheep (believers) must know and identify the true characteristics of a genuine shepherd. God requires faithfulness and truth. The Lord is the Chief Shepherd of those who believe in Him. If someone does not benefit from the Master Shepherd's care, it is because unbelief has removed the ability to hear the Lord's voice.

Sheep respond to the care of the Lord and His appointed shepherds by following. Their response to other voices that would lead astray must be to flee. The word *flee* comes from the Greek term *pheugo.* It indicates a decisive reaction in response to danger. The believer has a special relationship with the Lord and to the pastors who are true to Him.

The emphasis in this text is not on finding good pasture or healthy food. These goals are secondary to that of establishing a proper relationship with the shepherd. The believer's faith will draw him closer to this relationship and farther from those who would lead him astray. Many times other aspects of ministry, such as facilities and activities, rather than this committed relationship are emphasized. However, just as the sheep know the voice of the Chief Shepherd, the local church parishioner should be able to have an abiding confidence in his pastor.

The Guarding Shepherd (John 10:7-18)

Then said Jesus unto them again, Verily, verily, I say unto you, I am the door of the sheep. All that ever came before me are thieves and robbers: but the sheep did not hear them. I am the door: by me if any man enter in, he shall be saved, and shall go in and out, and find pasture (10:7-9).

In these verses, Jesus once again used the sheepfold to illustrate the nature of His shepherding and the standard for pastors. He portrayed the role of the shepherd as having the duty of guarding the sheepfold itself. This highlights his important role of protecting the sheep, which is even more important than nourishing the sheep. Before unprotected sheep starve, they will probably be killed by an intruder or an animal. Typically, the flock without a shepherd is in graver danger of slaughter than of malnourishment.

Again, Jesus contrasted His care to the violence that comes at the hands of thieves and robbers. Although they may have assumed the role of shepherds, the impostor shepherds' neglect makes them the same as thieves and robbers of the flock. Through their neglect of duty, violence comes to the flock. By contrast, the character of the true shepherd makes him also the guarding shepherd. He would be one who guarantees the all-important function of protection. This would in turn allow for the possibility of nourishment and pasture.

"The thief cometh not, but for to steal, and to kill, and to destroy: I am come that they might have life, and that they might have it more abundantly" (10:10). In this verse, Christ gives the most direct comparison between Himself and those who would do harm to the flock. The Lord does this by contrasting the essential goals of the shepherd and the thief. Christ's goal as the Good Shepherd is to bring abundant life to the sheep. *Abundant* comes from the Greek term *perisson.* It means "to be more than enough." The abundant life is one in which every need is supplied. The loving shepherd looks to the fulfillment, safety, and needs of the sheep.

By contrast, the aim of the thief is threefold. His first purpose is to *steal*—to remove the sheep from the safety and nurture of the flock and pasture. The second purpose is to *kill*—to remove life and resources from the sheep. The final purpose is the ultimate goal of the thief, to *destroy*, from the Greek word *apollumi*. It emphasizes violence, mangling, and mutilation of the sheep. The thief not only wanted to kill the sheep, he especially wanted to selfishly consume them.

Those opposed to the shepherding of the Lord have the profile of the thief. They seek to remove the members of a flock and lead them into heresy for a selfish goal. This is why the protecting function of the pastor is especially important.

I am the good shepherd: the good shepherd giveth his life for the sheep. But he that is an hireling, and not the shepherd, whose own the sheep are not, seeth the wolf coming, and leaveth the sheep, and fleeth: and the wolf catcheth them, and scattereth the sheep. The hireling fleeth, because he is an hireling, and careth not for the sheep (10:11-13).

This passage is central to the message of Christ as shepherd. Christ had just described the greatest threat to the sheep—that which would steal, kill, and destroy them. Now, in the face of the threat, Christ gave the one quality of the shepherd that is absolutely necessary if the sheep are to be protected—the giving of one's life for the sheep. Nevertheless, the emphasis on giving one's life does not disregard the importance of being on guard for his personal welfare as well as guarding the flock.

The term *giveth* comes from the Greek word *tithemi*. It emphasizes the offering of something. This is an intentional act and not the product of circumstance or necessity. The true shepherd is committed to giving his life for the sheep.

However, anyone who does not have this deep commitment is a hireling. The term *hireling* is translated from the Greek *misthotos* and is derived from a word meaning "wage." The term indicates someone who is merely seeking a wage. This is not an indictment against pastors who receive a salary. Rather, this passage emphasizes that the wage has become the shepherd's central concern. His improper focus leaves the sheep vulnerable.

Careth not indicates that the hireling does not dwell on or give concerned thought to the sheep in his care. He does not place great importance on the welfare of the flock. The amount of time dedicated to the thought and care of something indicates the degree of importance the individual places on it. The hireling has self-centered concerns and does not give the flock priority or care.

I am the good shepherd, and know my sheep, and am known of mine. As the Father knoweth me, even so know I the Father: and I lay down my life for the sheep (10:14,15).

Christ spoke of giving his life for the sheep in very personal terms. He gave His life out of a deep sense of loving relationship for the sheep. The term *know* indicates more than perception. It was not the same word used in the Greek text in verse 4 for perception. *Know* in verses 14 and 15 is translated from the Greek term *ginosko*, which stresses relationship. The loving relationship was an essential part of the sacrificial giving of His life for the sheep. It is out of this same kind of relationship that a pastor cares for a congregation today.

And other sheep I have, which are not of this fold: them also I must bring, and they shall hear my voice; and there shall be one fold, and one shepherd (10:16).

Christ continued to emphasize His love for the sheep by stressing reconciliation. Even though some of the sheep may have wandered from the fold, out of His mercy and love He would still call to them. His goal was reconciliation, that they would be drawn into His fold and know Him as shepherd. This emphasizes the need for the ministry of reconciliation. In the midst of the turmoil of protecting the flock from heresies, heretics, manipulators, deceivers, and so forth, the pastor must not lose compassion for those outside the fold. The pastoral call is always extended to them. The flock can be protected and a ministry of reconciliation conducted at the same time. This is Jesus' desire as expressed in verse 16.

"Therefore doth my Father love me, because I lay down my life, that I might take it again. No man taketh it from me, but I lay it down of myself. I have power to lay it down, and I have power to take it again. This commandment have I received of my Father" (10:17, 18).

In these verses, Christ summarized His relationship with the Father. While functioning as the Chief Shepherd of the church, Christ maintains a relationship with the heavenly Father. There are two essential parts to this relationship. The first is love. Christ emphasized this in verses 15-18. His love for the heavenly Father and His love for the flock are inseparably linked.

The second aspect of His relationship with the Father is obedience, the greater of the two. Obedience is the underlying and primary feature of the Father-Son relationship. Christ's office as Chief Shepherd over the church is manifested in acts of love done in obedience to the commands of the Father.

Obedience is the motivating factor for pastoral action. Acts of love for a congregation are initially birthed in obedience to the commands of the heavenly Father, not out of sociological or emotional necessity. Thus, pastoral action is founded in obedience to God's commands.

The Flock's Recognition of the True Shepherd (John 10:19-29)

> There was a division therefore again among the Jews for these sayings. And many of them said, He hath a devil, and is mad; why hear ye him? Others said, These are not the words of him that hath a devil. Can a devil open the eyes of the blind? And it was at Jerusalem the feast of the dedication, and it was winter. And Jesus walked in the temple in Solomon's porch. Then came the Jews round about him, and said unto him, How long dost thou make us to doubt? If thou be the Christ, tell us plainly (10:19-24).

The issue of spiritual perception is critical to the pastoral function. Only the sheep who know the voice of the Chief Shepherd are able to receive His pastoral care. Some of the Jews desired care. However, because of their unbelief, divisions and confusions continued among them. As a result, they did not receive the care of the Master. Neither can people in the church today receive pastoral care if they do not fully believe in the power and work of the Lord. No matter what a pastor does, or even Christ as the Chief Shepherd, without belief in Christ a person will not be able to recognize the loving pastoral care offered him.

"And I give unto them eternal life; and they shall never perish, neither shall any man pluck them out of my hand"

(10:28). The important task of shepherding believers encompasses not only the temporal but also the eternal needs of individuals. In this verse Christ again emphasized His care for the sheep. This time He emphasized His eternal care for the sheep. Without belief and perception, His care would be of no effect to them. They would not respond to nor hear His voice.

The Chief Shepherd Is God (John 10:30-38)

> I and my Father are one. . . . Say ye of him, whom the Father hath sanctified, and sent into the world, Thou blasphemest; because I said, I am the Son of God? If I do not the works of my Father, believe me not. But if I do, though ye believe not me, believe the works: That ye may know, and believe, that the Father is in me, and I in him (10:30,36-38).

The climactic purpose expressed in Ezekiel 34 was that the flock of God come to know that the Great Shepherd who watches over them is God and that they glorify and worship Him as God. The final and summary purpose was the same as when Christ described Himself as the Chief Shepherd of the believer. His desire is that the sheep come to know Him as God.

The recognition of the active, divine presence of God in the midst of the congregation is a primary purpose of pastoral action. It is the climax of the two major pastoral texts in both Testaments, Ezekiel 34 and John 10.

This recognition suffered at the hands of the self-serving shepherds in Ezekiel 34. Nevertheless, God himself intervened. In similar fashion, this recognition suffered at the hands of the disbelieving Pharisees. Yet Christ himself assured the man who was healed that He was the divine Chief Shepherd. The pastor and the local church fulfill the purposes of God to their greatest extent and come under the greatest amount of God's care when they recognize and believe in the presence and action of God himself in the midst of the flock. The work of the pastor and the church should seek this above all else.

The Call to Be a Pastor

3

The calling of the pastor is rooted in the authority of God (Isaiah 6; Amos 7; Ezekiel 2; Romans 10). The pastor's authority can be abused and distorted, and some attempt to manipulate it for selfish gain. Nevertheless, it is not a commission that begins in the minds of men. It comes from the compassion of God and by His command.

The basis of Isaiah's call was the voice of God. When Isaiah beheld the majesty of God (6:1-4), he was struck with conviction and confessed his sinfulness (v. 5). The Lord responded by purifying him and calling him into His service. Isaiah had a powerful ministry as a prophet but this ministry did not come merely from a burden he carried for humanity, or even for the nation of Israel. The Bible record shows clearly that Isaiah's calling came from God.

Amos' ministry also began with a commission from God. He was challenged by the king and religious authorities of Israel. He responded by clarifying why he was there. Amos explained that his calling had not come through family ties (7:14) but that it had come as a divine directive (v. 15). God commissioned him with a specific ministry and mission to Israel (v. 16).

The account of Ezekiel's powerful call to preach is given in chapter 2. God commissioned Ezekiel to preach despite the resistance of the people (vv. 2, 3). When Ezekiel spoke to the people, he clarified that the words of his prophecy were not human in origin (7:1, 2).

In the New Testament, the origin of the calling to the ministry of the preached Word is rooted in the direct commission of God. Paul stressed that the preached Word is essential for the development of faith (Romans 10:14). Paul clarified the origin of the preached Word—it is a sent Word (v. 15). The term *sent* implies the Word does not originate with the preacher. It is sent by God through the preacher. The calling and commission to preach the Word is of divine origin. In Scripture, the minister is seen as a vessel of God. His ministry is not the product of his own efforts.

Paul contended with men who abused the preaching of the gospel (Philippians 1:15-20). He wrote about individuals who had abused their privileges in the church and were doing damage to others (2 Timothy 3:1-10). However, the abuse of others did not divert Paul from claiming his call came directly from God (1 Timothy 1:1; 2 Timothy 1:1). The pastor and minister today must continue to make the same claim, despite the abuses the preaching of the gospel has suffered by others. It is far more perilous to claim a ministry has merely a human origin. The pastoral task certainly includes humanitarian effort; but as important as humanitarian efforts are, they are never sufficient in themselves to transform the life of a sinner into one that glorifies God. That is the work of the Holy Spirit, and the pastor must understand that to be effective for God's eternal kingdom, his pastoral activities must be imbued with the Spirit.

Overcoming Apathy (Philippians 2)

One issue confronting pastors in their ministry is apathy. At various times the minister may be discouraged about his calling. The compassion and zeal once felt for ministry may not be as strong as before. *Apathy* literally means "without motivation or drive." It is like a sailing ship with no wind to fill its sails. James Fowler, in his book *Stages of Faith*, asked concerning faith and motivation:

"What are you spending and being spent for? What commands and receives your best time, your best energy? What causes, dreams, goals or institutions are you pouring out your life for? As you live your life, what power or powers do you fear or dread? What power or powers do you rely on and trust? To what or whom are you committed in life? In death? With whom or what group do you share your most sacred and private hopes for your life and for the lives of those you love? What are those most sacred hopes, those most compelling goals and purposes in your life?"

What can bring the minister up from apathy? Richard Hoehn, in his book *Up From Apathy*, outlines steps that have moved individuals from apathy to action. The first step is confrontation—a life-changing experience so profound that it cannot be ignored. This is not merely a moment of intellectual awareness; rather, it is an experience that moves the individual's total being. The minister's calling may be just such an experience as this— whether it comes as a result of a single event, a series of events, or an eventual awareness. Remembering and rekindling this experience is important because it is the first formative event in moving an individual away from apathy and toward ministry.

Another step in moving away from apathy is a change in the individual's frame of reference—the way the person views the world. A call to ministry does indeed change the way an individual looks at life. A different perspective and deeper insight replace the old ways of thinking and behaving.

The example of Christ is especially helpful in understanding the transforming experience of one's calling. We cannot imagine an apathetic Christ—either toward the needs of the world or His call from the Father. Christ took the step of sacrifice—He made himself of "no reputation" (Philippians 2:7). In similar fashion, the calling of a minister to service requires sacrifice. Without reconciliation to this requirement, the minister will remain in apathy. When the giving of oneself sacrificially in ministry diminishes, the potential for apathy becomes greater.

Christ took also a step toward servanthood: He took on "the form of a servant" (v. 7). A further step was humility: In fulfilling His calling, He "humbled himself" (v. 8). And Christ took the ultimate step of obedience: He was "obedient unto death" (v. 8). Christ had a calling from the heavenly Father, and He responded to it willingly. No hint of apathy is associated with Christ. He chose to sacrifice, become a servant, humble Himself, and be obedient in order to fulfill His divine mission.

It is important to note that moving away from apathy is based on the decisions of the one called into ministry. The pastor's call is a life-changing experience that requires the minister to respond with sacrifice, servanthood, humility, and obedience. A divine calling requires a personal response to an experience initiated by God.

The Fear of Failure (Luke 11:37—12:12)

In Luke 11 and 12, Christ and the disciples were criticized by the Pharisees. The Pharisees had gained considerable support in their effort to discredit the Lord and His disciples (see 12:1). While the disciples were feeling pressure from the multitude, Jesus ministered to them about confidence in ministry. The disciples were confronted with assaults that threatened the success of their ministry efforts. Jesus faced this badgering too. In the midst of adversity, He taught the disciples the key to combating such oppression.

Jesus told the disciples the key to facing threats either spoken or implied was to fear God and His wrath more than they feared the abuse of the crowd (12:4, 5). The Pharisees paid greater attention to external actions than to the internal condition of the heart (11:39; 12:1-3).

Fear of failure comes from overattention to the external pressures of ministry. Sometimes the minister allows these forces to influence him more than the internal power of Christ's Spirit. The fear of man at the expense of one's fear of God creates the fear of failure in ministry.

Jesus exhorted the disciples to base their ministry, especially when it came to facing danger or stress, on an awesome fear of and reverence for God and His sovereignty. The ministry of the Holy Spirit within them would create the confidence they would need and provide them with guidance during critical times of oppression (12:11, 12). Thus, a ministry that is rooted in the fear of the Lord will overcome external pressures.

Conflict (John 7:1-31)

This section of Scripture shows how Jesus personally responded to opposing forces and tells of the decisions He made concerning His calling and ministry. The disciples were encouraging Jesus to avoid conflict with the Pharisees. The Feast of Tabernacles was taking place and the disciples were fearful of a confrontation with the religious authorities in Jerusalem. Jesus did not want to clash with the Pharisees, but neither did He want to avoid a ministry opportunity ordained by the Father (John 7:1-9).

Jesus explained to the disciples the importance of depending on the heavenly Father for direction. The timing of His actions was directed by the Father (7:6-10). This required a dependency upon the guidance of the heavenly Father. At times, the issues of conflict in ministry revolve around circumstances. In those times, it is important to focus on the direction of the heavenly Father. This was Jesus' concern.

Because of Jesus' sensitivity to the Father, He taught in Jerusalem at just the right time. He did not ignore the circumstances. There were Jews present who had previously threatened Him. Jesus was not being foolish or blind about the threats. He was responding to the leading of the Father rather than being coerced by those who threatened Him (7:11-14). The outcome was that the Jews did not persecute Him; in fact, they marveled at His ministry (7:15).

Jesus did not take credit for His perception in His dealing with the circumstances. Rather, He testified about His faithful obedience and that He followed the will of the Father (7:16-18, 28, 29). Jesus was able to continue His ministry and bring glory to the Father because He overcame the resistance of the Pharisees by heeding the timing and direction of the Father (7:30, 31).

The pastor cannot afford to ignore circumstances, especially those which may be perilous to himself, his family, or the local congregation. These conditions must be taken into serious account and not ignored. Nevertheless, the primary motivation and direction for action must come ultimately from one's sense of God's direction. This was the issue Jesus took into consideration in John 7. The disciples encouraged Him to pay attention to the circumstances. And Jesus did not ignore the circumstances, but He clarified that His course of action was determined by the Father.

Ministerial Ethics and Personal Conduct

God's Representation Through Creation

The personal conduct of a minister has a strong impact on pastoral ministry. The local congregation and the community observe the conduct of the minister every day. Even more important is the personal conduct a minister displays before the family. This section will look at the theological reasons and motivations for the minister's personal conduct, which is a vital part of every aspect of the pastor's life.

God has continually been involved in the world of His creation. He is its Creator and sustainer (Isaiah 40). God did not merely create the world and then leave it to run by itself. In turn, the world reflects the involvement of the Creator. God is constantly involved in the affairs of mankind. We, along with all of nature, were created to give glory and honor to Him (Genesis 1, 2; Romans 1).

Scripture reveals the personal involvement of God with man even before the coming of Christ into the world. The record of events in the lives of those who lived before the Flood, the patriarchs, the monarchs of Israel and Judah, the prophets, and the people of His holy nation describes His active involvement. The Scriptures themselves are a testimony of God's involvement in the lives of the people of the earth, for He himself inspired the written record of His dealings with them and His communications to them.

God further revealed Himself through the Incarnation, becoming flesh and dwelling among men. Christ represented God the Father on earth. The works of the Lord were not merely His own; they were also the will of the Father (John 17:4). God intended that He be glorified through the Son.

Implied in the fact of God's active representation and involvement in the world is His intention that all creation magnify Him. The world and all of its substance were created to bring to Him the glory and honor due Him. This includes the ministry and personal conduct of the pastor. God has chosen to represent Himself in this world through those He has created. Creation is not an end in itself; all creatures bear the responsibility of glorifying and representing their Creator (Romans 1).

Christian Influence in the World

The principle of God's representation in the world is especially seen in the incarnation of Christ. When Christ came into the world in the form of humanity, He became "God with us" (Matthew 1:23). This representation of God in Christ is carried through the believer to the world by the presence of Christ within. This means that just as Christ represented the Father, so does the believer represent God in Christ to the world.

This places a responsibility on every believer to faithfully carry out this task of representation. The believer is an epistle, a living document, before others (2 Corinthians 3:2). The Christian bears the message of redemption to the world, heralding its truth (Romans 10). In the giving of the Holy Spirit, God intended that the Spirit-filled believer be a witness, testimony, and representative to others (Acts 2).

The pastor's place as a creation of God, as a representative of the Lord in his life, and as a role model for his congregation all require of him the best possible personal conduct and ministry.

Representation of God in the World

The Christian's focus in personal conduct and code of ethics must be to imitate Christ. Paul warned about lifestyles and conduct not centered in Christ (Colossians 2). Legalism could easily become the focus, basing one's conduct on the rules of men rather than on Christ. The primary responsibility of the Christian's life is to present the humility, love, and service of Christ to others.

The representation of Christ in the world must especially be evident within the body of believers. Christ told the disciples that a new commandment would govern them, which would be the love they would have toward one another (John 13:34, 35). Their obedience to this command would represent Christ to the world. The life the believer lives among the body of believers is especially important for this reason.

This accentuates the importance of the ethics of the minister within the church. Not only does the pastor represent God as one of His creations and as a born-again believer, but the pastor must also participate in the representation of Christ as revealed through the church.

The church is the primary means Christ has chosen to reveal the mystery of God. Christ died for the church and gave the Holy Spirit to believers in the church. Life in the Spirit is especially revealed in the context of the church; thus the pastor must integrate his life with the life of the church. The pastor is especially viewed as a representative of God in his personal actions and ethics.

The pastor is not the only person participating in the life of the church, of course. The other believers also reveal the power of God through their life and conduct. However, the pastor serves as a shepherd; therefore, the pastor's witness is not merely an individual one. The pastor is a particularly visible representative of God, because he is a shepherd of those endeavoring to represent God to the world.

Representing God in Ministry

The pastor's personal conduct and code of ethics can be analyzed through comparison to individuals in other professions. This is not to say that ministry is merely a profession. However, pastors do have similarities to those in the community who are uniquely committed to certain secular vocations. The lawyer belongs to a profession dedicated to upholding and interpreting the law. Doctors are members of a profession dedicated to maintaining the health of individuals. Bankers are part of a profession dedicated to the financial stability and prosperity of the community. Pastors are committed to a calling ordained to fulfill the will of God in and for the world.

Each of the professions mentioned above have certain standards of certification which monitor the private and professional conduct of its members. For example, lawyers are credentialed and monitored by the American Bar Association; doctors, by the American Medical Association. These organizations require their members' conduct to uphold the standards and principles to which the profession is dedicated. If a lawyer, even in private conduct, should violate a principle of client privacy or the standards of the law, the lawyer's standing with the profession would be in jeopardy.

The pastor is also committed to the standards of conduct set forth in Scripture. Throughout history, denominations and movements have been organized to uphold standards of conduct. The conduct of the minister, even in his personal life, is subject to the standards set by Scripture and those bodies of the church committed to upholding those standards.

The pastor's life is not his own. God has fashioned the minister to represent Him as a part of His creation. As a believer, the pastor has a responsibility to see that his conduct conforms to the example of Christ in order that his life may demonstrate the presence of Christ within. As a member of the body of Christ, the pastor is bound to the corporate reflection of Christ. The pastor must live in such a way that He represents the presence and power of the Lord in his life and in the church.

The Offices and Gifts of Ministry

4

The pastor must have a clear concept of the place of the church in pastoral ministry. This conception is based on a perception of the active work of God's sovereignty within the church. The pastor must then see that God has called the church into existence. God is not only active, but He has chosen the church as the primary vehicle through which He operates in this world. The perception of God's work and the instrumentality of the church is vital for effective pastoral ministry.

The church is not merely an instrument to aid and assist humanity, though the church may do things that improve the condition of the people. However, the motivation behind the action of the church is divine. The church is led by the direction of the Lord. In fact, the Lord is already active within and through the church.

This chapter will build around God's active sovereignty, that is, His action within the church. The first priority is His active sovereignty. Next, the concept of the "gathered church" will be discussed. The gathered church is the means by which God reveals His fullness today (Ephesians

3; 4). Finally, the role of gifts, offices, and needs will be presented as the agenda of God's action through the gathered church.

Primacy of God's Action

What is the first and foremost question the church must ask itself? This might be called the "first question" of the church. Whatever you say this "first question" is reveals what you perceive to be the center and source of all that the church does. What is the absolute center of all that the church does and is about? What is the origin, the source, of all that the church does and claims? This last question is also related to what is the ultimate conclusion or goal of the church.

"What are the needs of the people?" is a possible first question. However, the problem with this as the first question is that it places the people at the center and origin of the church.

"What can I do to minister to the people?" is another possible first question. Yet the problem with this as the first question is that it places the minister at the center of the church.

"What can we do to minister together?" is another possible first question. Still, the problem is that this places you and me at the center and source of the church.

"What is God doing?" is the compelling first question for the church. God and His action is at the center and origin of the church. Nothing else forms the center and source of the church. The church in all that it does must constantly ask before any other concern, "What is God doing?"

"What do I hope God will do?" is not the same as

"What is God doing?" The church cannot accurately know what to do until it can at least begin to perceive what God is doing. The action of the church cannot lead or even parallel what God is doing. The action of the church must follow the action of God.

The first priority of the church is to perceive what God is doing in the church, that is, His active sovereignty. God is active, and He is God; that is, He is sovereign. Hence, God's action can be called His active sovereignty. The perception of His active sovereignty is the core from which ministry is launched. Once the church perceives God's action, then its personnel, programs, and priorities must be built around His action.

In considering the activity of God within the church, an important feature to understand is that God intended that His people gather together. The church is not a group of individuals going separate ways. Rather, the church is to be marked by unity and love (John 13:34, 35). A powerful description of God's working through the church as it gathered together is in the Book of Acts. It is clear from this record of the early church in action that it gathered to accomplish the work of God.

This might seem like an obvious or simplistic point. However, the gathering of the church is more important than any single individual. It is also more important than any ideal or goal. The gathered church is larger than any threat it may encounter.

Without a clear understanding of the necessity for the church to gather together, the work of the pastor will be less than effective. This is because God has chosen to work among His people as they gather together. God's active sovereignty in the midst of the assembled church can be diagramed as follows:

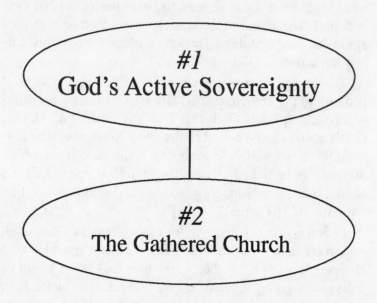

God's Action and the Gathered Church
(These items occur in the order listed.)

1. God is active in all parts of the church as the center and origin.

2. God works through the church as it gathers together.

The church cannot be confined within the walls of a building. Neither does the church exist only when its members are assembled. However, the abiding unity of the church mandates the assembling together in one place for fellowship and worship. And when the church is not physically in one place, there is still that sense of unity and love among its people.

This chapter looks at the example of the church in Acts. It was a "gathering" church. Their togetherness brought strength to their ministry. The gathering of the church will also be considered in light of its implications for the local pastor's calling to ministry.

The Church Gathered for Fellowship, Worship, and Blessing

The gathered church received Jesus' final teachings on earth (Acts 1:4). Then, obeying His instructions, they gathered together and received the blessings Christ had promised them (Acts 1:12-14; 2:1-4). When the blessings and power of the Spirit came on the Day of Pentecost, it came to the assembled body of believers.

Private times of devotion are important for every believer, but the pattern of also gathering together for worship, teaching, and waiting on the Lord is clearly seen in Acts. The Lord loves to bless His people as He did on the Day of Pentecost when they were gathered together in unity (see Psalm 133).

The Church Gathered in Response to Persecution

At times the early church encountered severe persecution. This was the case in Acts 5. The church gathered for prayer in response to the persecution. They both prayed for and encouraged one another. Their standing together in unity was especially important because this was the very point at which their critics expected them to fail. Gamaliel in particular had stated that the dissolution of the church would be evidence it was not legitimate by God's standards (Acts 5:34-39).

The church today is still encouraged and strengthened by gathering together. The pastor must be able to recognize the strength gained by the church's banding together. When persecution is so severe that it poses a physical threat, it is more difficult to meet together. However, the Book of Acts, as well as subsequent church history, documents that when believers assemble in spite of physical danger, not only are the believers strengthened and encouraged, but also the preaching of the gospel continues to win many converts to Christ. The gathering together of the early church believers was convincing proof of the validity of their spiritual experience before a skeptical world.

The Church Gathered to Minister to Others and to One Another

The ministry potential of the gathering church is seen throughout Acts. A wonderful example is in the account of the blessing and ministry that came to Cornelius' house. A group of spiritually hungry people had gathered together in Cornelius' home, eager to hear from Peter what God wanted them to do. Their hunger and their submissiveness paid off; they received the Holy Spirit baptism.

The ministry potential of today's church is greatly enhanced when the church gathers in His name. Whether in the sanctuary of the church or in a home prayer group, the ministry of the saints to one another is a vital part of every gathering of believers.

The Church Gathered for Missionary and Evangelistic Work

The church has the mission and calling to reach the world. This call to evangelize the lost is part of Christ's commission to every believer. The church in the Book of Acts carried this out, not only as individuals but also as the unified church. Paul was an excellent example of one person mightily used by the Lord. However, the assembled church played an essential role in the work of missions and evangelism. Paul was commissioned by the gathered church (Acts 13), he remained in contact with the body of believers between his missionary journeys (14:27), and he submitted himself and his ministry to the government of the church in conference (ch. 15). No matter what he did individually, the community of believers was still a necessary part of his missionary and evangelistic ministry.

The corporate church still plays a vital role in the work of missions and evangelism. This does not negate but rather complements the individual believer's call to minister in other parts of the world. The gathered church is a resource for missionary and evangelistic ministries. The pastor, in organizing outreach and evangelism ministries, must encourage the local church to participate with prayer support and financial means.

The Church Gathered to Solve Internal Problems

A number of problems arose in the early church which at times appeared to threaten the very existence of the church. Nevertheless, the church continued because of the power of Christ. When the church addressed these problems, it did so as the gathered church, not as isolated individuals. Two important examples of the aggregate church functioning in this manner come from Acts 6, when there was murmuring among the Grecian Christians, and from Acts 15, where the question concerning the requirements for Gentile converts arose. In each case the church gathered together to resolve issues.

At times, a pastor and congregation may be tempted to try to solve the problems within the body of believers by remaining quiet, expecting each person to resolve the problem in his own way. However, when problems arise that affect the whole congregation, the church needs the strength of the unified body to find a solution. In fact, this is the pastoral pattern established by the apostles in the Book of Acts.

The Church Gathered for Times of Commissioning

Some individuals in the early church had special calls on their lives for specific ministries, but the gathered church still played a role in their ministries. Although the calling was to an individual, the church still felt it was important for the minister and his ministry to be affirmed by the body of believers. This process of affirmation had its roots in the Old Testament (Numbers 27:18-23; Deuteronomy 34:9) and was part of the commissioning of workers described in Acts 6:1-6. Paul also referred to this practice in 1 Timothy 4:14.

The affirmation of the ministry of individual members by the body of Christ is an important function of the gathered church. Times of commissioning of workers or the ordination of ministers can communicate support, confidence in, and care for the ministers and their ministries. Further, it is a spiritual commitment carried out in both Old and New Testaments by God's people.

The concept of the gathered church is vital to understanding the calling of the pastor. Calling into ministry incorporates and represents a relationship with the gathered church. The pastor's calling is affirmed within the context of the gathered church.

The gathered church represents a dimension that goes beyond individuality and personal concerns. It represents the covenant community of the Old Testament and witnesses to the oneness of the Trinity by maintaining unity with one another (John 17). The common good of the entire church has often been sacrificed at the altar of individualistic goals and concerns. The church functions at its optimum when its members come together in unity. The fact that individuals meet together in one place does not guarantee togetherness. Essential for having concord is love and the desire to be one in spirit (John 13:34-35; John 17).

Offices of Ministry in the Church

As the church in New Testament gathered, it did not depend on organizational principles derived from purely human rationale. Rather, the operation and organization of the church centered on the gifts and offices given to the church by the Lord. This does not preclude the organizational ability of individuals. However, the organization and structure of a church must be built upon a certain foundation. Gifts and offices given by the Lord are the foundation of the organization of the church.

God's action operates in the midst of the church as it gathers in love and oneness. Gifts and offices are exercised within the framework of God's action and the unity of the church. Spiritual gifts are the enabling power within those who function in these capacities within the framework of the church. Offices are functions carried out by those who have been enabled by the spirit. These gifts and offices in turn meet needs presented by the Lord. This process is illustrated on the following page. The order as well as the arrangement of the elements of this diagram is important. (1) The process must begin with God's action as the center and the origin of the church. (2) God's action works through the gathered church. (3) Only then can we understand that individuals are gifted by God within the context of the gathered church. (4) Offices are then for the functioning of gifts from God. (5) Finally, God makes needs apparent to the church, especially when the church is following His action.

The Source of Spiritual Gifts

God gives gifts to individuals for the empowerment of the body of Christ. When spiritual gifts are discussed in Scripture, their origin is especially emphasized. The result of the operation of a particular gift may be of particular significance and bring great benefits to an individual or group of people; however, the substance of the gift itself must remain secondary to the importance we place on the bestower of the gift—God himself. The origin of a spiritual gift is what makes it divine. The content of a gift, however great its benefits may be, does not make it divine; it is divine because it comes from God. His action is the center and origin of the gift.

Paul wrote much of what we know about the operation of spiritual gifts. That he emphasized the giver of the gifts above the gifts themselves is especially evident in 1 Corinthians 12:1-11. Paul stressed that spiritual gifts come by means of the Spirit of God. He conveyed this principle seven times in verses 4-11.

God's Action and the Gathered Church
(These items occur in the order listed.)
1. God is active in all parts of the church as the center and origin.
2. God works through the church as it gathers together.
3. God gifts individuals through His power.
4. Gifts need functions and offices for organization and effectiveness.
5. God makes various needs within and outside the church apparent.

The various phrases Paul used to describe the essential role of the Spirit reveal different emphases concerning the origin and guidance of the gifts. The phrase "by the Spirit" that is found four times in verses 3 and 9 is from the Greek phrase *en pneumati*. It indicates the instrumental means by which these gifts are made possible.

The phrase "by the same Spirit" occurs in verse 8. It is from the Greek phrase *dia tou pneumatos* and emphasizes that the cause of the manifestation of the gifts is the Spirit. The same phrase, "by the same Spirit," also occurs a second time in the same verse. This second time, different terms are used in the Greek text—*kata to auto pneuma*—which emphasize that the limits and guidance of the gifts are directed by the Spirit.

These different phrases indicate that the instrumental means, originating cause, and guiding limits of the gifts are all "by the Spirit." Paul listed the gifts by name but did not give extensive definitions for them. He stressed instead that they are gifts bestowed through the ministry of the Spirit.

Throughout 1 Corinthians 12, Paul declared that the gifts are given. They are not self-generated abilities and talents. They are given by God. Paul's usage of the word *given* indicates a continued operation. In other words, the gifts continue to be given by God. At no point do they originate with man; their source is God himself.

The Relationship Between Gifts and Offices

Spiritual gifts are given to carry out the functions necessary for the operation of the church. Paul exhorted the Corinthian believers to use their spiritual gifts for the work of edifying the body of believers: "Even so ye, forasmuch as ye are zealous of spiritual gifts, seek that ye may excel to the edifying of the church" (1 Corinthians 14:12).

The motivation and insight necessary to edify the body is an essential work of the Holy Spirit for the enabling of individuals for ministry within the body of Christ. The New Testament affirms that the work of edifying the body is accomplished through the divine move of God. Many times the Spirit of God speaks directly to a person. At other times, the Spirit enables someone else to help through the power of the Holy Spirit.

This does not mean that human talents and abilities are not used; rather, they play an important role, and they become a vital part of ministry within the body as they are yielded to and transformed by the power of the Spirit. However, the Spirit also imparts supernatural gifts so that the work of the church may be carried out. If the Spirit is not operative to enable and give spiritual gifts to individuals in the church, then the work of the church is just another of society's humanitarian efforts.

The work of the Spirit enables individuals to perform certain tasks, or *offices*. These offices are not to be viewed so much as positions as functions intended to glorify the Lord and edify the church. Not everyone has the same function in the body of Christ. As a result, certain distinctions and differences in function are inevitable. These must be identified and fostered in the life of the church.

The offices of ministry have the same source as the gifts. They originate with God. They are not merely the product of human organizational necessity. Divine in origin, they are established for the purpose of facilitating the enabling power of the gifts of the Spirit. The ministry of the gifts becomes functional through the form of the offices.

This does not mean that only those holding a particular office have spiritual gifts. Many times spiritual gifts operate through individuals who hold no designated office within the body of believers. However, everyone who holds an office should have the enabling power of the Spirit within.

Offices in the Functioning of the Church

Some of the offices given attention in the New Testament include apostle, prophet, evangelist, pastor/teacher, deacon, elder, and overseer. Each has a special emphasis of ministry and function within the body of Christ. None of them carries more significance than another. Their importance is equal, while their function is different. The function of the office is its most important feature. The divine calling for each office comes from the same source. Although none is more important than another, the function of each is distinct.

The term *apostle* comes from the Greek term *apostolos*, which means "one sent forth on a certain mission." Not only was the individual sent, but a specific and unique mission was also to be carried out. This is why the 12 apostles are in a different category from others who have ministered since that time. They were given a distinct ministry to carry out by the Savior. For example, the apostle Paul was sent on the unique mission of being an apostle to the Gentiles.

The term *prophet* comes from the Greek term *prophetes*, which emphasizes the "presentation of a word before/unto others." It is used to refer to those who were given insight into future events, to declare them. Also, the term referred to those who declared the Word of the Lord, especially in times when the Word would be resisted. In all these cases, the people needed to hear from God. These usages are evident in both Testaments. In the church today, all these functions are operative as well.

Evangelist comes from the Greek term *euaggelistes.* It means "messenger of glad tidings." The term emphasizes the bearing of the good news of the gospel, especially that people may come to a saving knowledge of the Lord.

The office of pastor/teacher came from its usage in Ephesians 4:11. The Greek term for *teacher* is *didaskalos.* It refers not only to the transmission of knowledge and information but also to the process of guiding and leading others. It includes a mentoring and training process that affects the very lives of others.

Deacon comes from the Greek term *diakonos,* which emphasizes work that ministers to the temporal, common needs of others. It was used to refer to those who waited on tables and served others. The word could refer to either slaves or royal stewards. The use of the word in reference to the church indicates action that was done in representation of Christ. The work of the deacon was not merely an act of service; it was something done in order to reflect the servant spirit of Christ. The term was constructed from two Greek terms—*dia*, meaning "through," and *konos*, meaning "common." The term meant "through the common" and emphasized the ability to do something by using common means and ordinary things. In the case of the gospel, *diakonos* implies the ability to spread the gospel through common means. The particular use of the word could refer to slaves or royal stewards. The particular use of the word in the church indicated action that was done in representation of Christ through the methods of a common nature.

The work of the deacon was not merely an act of service; it was something done in order to reflect the servant spirit of Christ by using means common to everyone.

Elder is translated from the Greek term *presbuteros*. A basic form of the word *presbus*, stressed the age of an individual. The term became synonymous with someone who was respected because of maturity and experience. The person also was considered, if not in fact appointed, as a representative of others. The church viewed elders as persons of maturity, worthy of emulation. They presided over many of the affairs of the church. They provided leadership and, at times, instruction.

Overseer is translated from the Greek term *episkopos*. It refers to "one who gives oversight, protection, and guardianship to others—hovering over or covering them." Protection is a major focus of the office of overseer—the watchful care of a loving and benevolent protector. In this role he is at times the defender of those under his care, both inside and outside the church.

The Standard of Ephesians 4:1-16

The Context of Spiritual Gifts and Offices

Ephesians 4 is especially helpful in understanding the pattern of God's sovereign actions in the church. This pasage reveals God's intention for the church—unity (vv. 1-6). It also shows God uses gifts and offices to minister to and to equip the church for ministry.

These principles are helpful in understanding pastoral theology. They stress that God is active in the church. The pastor and congregation must strive to be aware of and understand God's action in their midst. God has given gifts, abilities, and offices to the church; and He has given these in order that His will and power be revealed through the body of believers.

"I therefore, the prisoner of the Lord, beseech you that ye walk worthy of the vocation wherewith ye are called" (v. 1). This is the opening verse of the section in Ephesians where Paul gave practical application to the theological concerns he had discussed previously. He began with a warm exhortation. *Beseech* is translated from a Greek word which means to "call someone alongside." Paul was calling the readers to his side to offer them this exhortation.

The central focus of his exhortation is to "walk worthy." *Walk* indicates one's manner of living—one's conduct. It emphasizes the practical side of life. *Worthy* is translated from the Greek word *axios*, which meant to be weighed or balanced by a standard. In this verse, the standard is the *vocation* to which one has been called.

The *vocation* of Christians means they are are divinely called by God. The Christian, according to Paul, is to conduct himself in a manner corresponding with that calling. The nature of that divine call is the topic of chapters 1-3. The implications of that call for the Christian and for the church is the topic of chapters 4-6. "With all lowliness and meekness, with longsuffering, forbearing one another in love; endeavouring to keep the unity of the Spirit in the bond of peace" (4:2, 3).

The life of the church is directly related to the strength of individual believers. The pastor must be concerned not only for the strength of the church as a whole but also for the strength of individual believers. In this light, Paul emphasized the strength of the individual along with the maturity of the entire body of believers. Verses 2 and 3 address the growth of the individual believer as a prelude to the exhortations concerning the church.

In the first part of verse 2, Paul indicated the walk the believer is to have. This description is threefold. First, it is to be with "all lowliness." The word for *lowliness* in the Greek text meant humility of heart. It means to subject "oneself to others and to be more concerned about their welfare than one's own" (Walter Grundmann, *Theological Dictionary of the New Testament*).

The second description of the walk the believer is to follow is *meekness*, which in this context means "the humble and gentle attitude which expresses itself in a patient submissiveness to offense, free from malice and desire for revenge" (*Linguistic Key to the Greek New Testament*).

The final description of the kind of walk Christians are to follow is *long-suffering*. This word in the Greek referred to a person's long endurance in the face of raging opposition and anger from others.

After this threefold description, Paul connected these requirements for individuals with the call of the Lord to the church. He described God's purpose for all believers. This call is not for individuals alone; it also applies to all members of the body of Christ collectively.

"There is one body, and one Spirit, even as ye are called in one hope of your calling; one Lord, one faith, one baptism, one God and Father of all, who is above all, and through all, and in you all" (4:4-6). Paul exhorted the believers that the goal of the Christian's individual walk is directed toward unity with God and with other believers. No Christian can live the Christian life alone. Christianity requires concern for others. The principles of the Christian walk are lived out in relationship to others.

Unity with other believers is vitally connected to unity with God. Christ prayed on the nisght of His betrayal that believers would be one and that they would be one with Him (John 17). This is the essence of Paul's exhortation here. The goal of the Christian walk is achieved through oneness with God and with other believers. It is toward this end that Paul began to introduce the topic of spiritual gifts and offices.

The Purpose of Spiritual Gifts and Offices

"But unto every one of us is given grace according to the measure of the gift of Christ" (4:7). In this verse, Paul identified the source of the unity, gifts, and offices of the church. It is the grace given by Christ, and this grace is the gift that makes the other gifts possible in the church. The foundation of the work of the church can be traced to it. Out of this gift the operation of the church flows.

"Wherefore he saith, When he ascended up on high, he led captivity captive, and gave gifts unto men. (Now that he ascended, what is it but that he also descended first into the lower parts of the earth? He that descended is the same also that ascended up far above all heavens, that he might fill all things)" (vv. 8-10).

The channel through which the grace of Christ flows is the work of Christ. Christ brought His grace to the believer and the church through His life and work. This included His ministry, death, burial, and resurrection. God's grace is a gift granted to the believer and the church. The phrase "fill all things" refers not only to the accomplished work of Christ in the believer and to Christ's fulfillment of prophecy but also to His work for the church. The work of Christ is the ministry of grace that makes possible the gifts and offices of the church.

"And he gave some, apostles; and some, prophets; and some, evangelists; and some, pastors and teachers" (4:11). The offices listed here are the result of the grace of God and His work through Christ. The church began as a result of the grace and work of Christ, and His work and grace provide the very foundation for the functioning of the church. This principle applies to all functions of the church, whether they are administrative, teaching, or pastoral functions, and they include worship leadership, service ministries, and evangelism.

The Greek text is so constructed that the mention of "pastors and teachers" actually reflects two different aspects of the same function. A pastor is also a teacher and a teacher must also be a shepherd. The best example of this is Christ, the Chief Shepherd. He is also the great teacher of His disciples and all those who follow Him.

"For the perfecting of the saints, for the work of the ministry, for the edifying of the body of Christ: till we all come in the unity of the faith, and of the knowledge of the Son of God, unto a perfect man, unto the measure of the stature of the fulness of Christ" (vv. 12, 13).

The word *for* in verse 12 indicates that what follows is the purpose for what preceded in verse 11. That is, the gifts listed in verse 11 are for the reasons cited in verses 12 and 13. Paul presented the perfecting of the saints as the general purpose for the bestowal of these gifts. Following this, he gave a fivefold description of that perfecting work. This is a description of the ultimate goal of the gifts and offices God has given to function in the church. Paul gave an abbreviated version of this goal in 1 Corinthians 14:12

when he used the phrase "edifying of the church." In Ephesians 4:12-16 he expanded this objective.

These gifts given by God are to the members of the body of Christ. *Perfecting* in verse 12 is translated from the Greek word *katartismos* and is a different word from the one translated "perfect" in verse 13. The word used in verse 12 means "to prepare something or someone to be ready at the suitable time." The word is used for the outfitting of buildings, furniture, or persons. It is even used as a medical term in reference to properly repairing or setting a broken bone. The gifts and offices are to be used to prepare and equip the members of the body.

This perfecting is to extend into five areas. The first area is "for the work of the ministry." This refers to Christian service. The second area is "for the edifying of the body of Christ." *Edifying* is literally "house building." It emphasizes here the building up of others. The third area is that "we all come in the unity of the faith, and of the knowledge of the Son of God." The emphasis here is not on unanimity alone, but it speaks of a unity that is characterized by faith and the knowledge of Christ. The fourth area is the goal of a "perfect man." *Perfect* here means maturity, completeness, or being full-grown. The reference is to spiritual growth and maturity.

The final area the gifts are to attain in believers is that we grow "unto the measure of the stature of the fulness of Christ." This is the climactic goal of the gifts, that the believer will be fashioned in the image of Christ. Paul was careful to describe the degree to which the believer is to strive. This measure is "the stature," or full extent, of the "fulness of Christ." Christ is the standard of maturity for Christians individually and collectively.

The reason God is active in the church, the reason He has given gifts to enable the functions of the church, the reason God has given offices to carry out the functions of the church, is to perfect the saints in the church. That perfection is set according to the standard of Christ himself.

2

MINISTERING, EQUIPPING, AND BEING A PART OF THE PEOPLE OF GOD

The Pastor and the Ministry of the Laity

5

This chapter will focus on trends and patterns of pastoral development and church administration observed in the New Testament. In particular, the organization of the laity for effective service will be emphasized. These organizational principles represent the church as a living organism responsive to God and the needs of others, as well as the gifts God has given to the body of believers.

Responsive to Needs (Acts 6:1-8)

In the New Testament, the laity directed its ministry efforts toward the needs of others. This included needs within the body of believers as well as those outside the church. The early church was a ministering body, concerned about the spiritual and physical welfare of others.

It was the practice of the early church to provide assistance to the widows in need among them. A dispute arose between the Grecian and Hebrew members of the church because they felt this assistance was not being administered equally between the two groups. The church then took action to organize in such a way as to meet the widows' needs fairly. In spite of the dispute, the church kept the widows' needs as a primary concern. Because the church remembered its dual responsibility—to preach the Word and to care for the needy—the result was that the overall ministry and outreach of the church prospered (vv. 7, 8). When a church focuses on meeting the needs of the poor, it will be blessed.

Gifts of the Spirit Rather Than Human Ability (Ephesians 4:1-16)

Christ, through His work and grace, has given gifts to the church (vv. 7, 8). These gifts serve to equip the church in its functions and offices (vv. 11-16). No mention is made of mere human ingenuity or ability. The work of the church does not depend primarily on human ability; it depends on what the church receives from God. Furthermore, the work of the church does not represent the collective ability of a group of individuals. Human ability is seen only in light of how it can serve God and be used of Him.

Character Qualifications Given Greater Attention Than Human Abilities

"Wherefore, brethren, look ye out among you seven men of honest report, full of the Holy Ghost and wisdom, whom we may appoint over this business" (Acts 6:3).

The criteria the church used to select workers were character, spirituality, and wisdom. Ability to perform a task is never sufficient of itself to be selected for a ministry position. The enabling of the Holy Spirit is always necessary to perform a spiritual task, no matter how innately talented an individual may be.

Exodus 35—39 gives principles for the selection and use of leaders and workers. In these chapters, God gave instructions for both the materials to be used and the actual construction of the tabernacle.

The descriptions of the workers and leaders to be selected emphasized inner quality and spiritual maturity. Some of the descriptions include "of a willing heart" (35:5), "willing hearted" (v. 22), "whom his spirit made willing" (v. 21), "whose heart stirred them up in wisdom" (v. 26), and "whose heart made them willing" (v. 29). These terms meant that they were to be people who were not only able but also discerning (wise), who had a volunteer spirit (willing), who possessed adequate motivation (stirred), and who possessed inner maturity and spirituality (heart).

Process of Endorsement and Oversight (Acts 15, 16)

Paul used a system of oversight and administration for the churches he planted. He did not leave them to themselves but administered them systematically by communicating with them, requiring certain things of them, and making regular visits to them. This process of oversight shows the necessity for practical responsibility and accountability in the organization of the laity *(laos)*, "the people of God."

The apostles at Jerusalem also exercised administrative oversight. Acts 10, 11, 15 and 16 specifically record occasions when the ministries of Peter and Paul were held accountable by the council at Jerusalem. This process helped the church to maintain unity as it grew. The church's concerns were both spiritual, dealing with issues such as salvation and receiving the baptism in the Spirit, and practical, dealing with practices in the daily lives of members and the administration of ordinances and practices in the church.

Commissioning of Workers (Acts 6:6)

"Whom they set before the apostles: and when they had prayed, they laid their hands on them" (6:6).

The church conducted a special time of commissioning for the workers they had selected to oversee the distribution to meet the needs of the widows. The commissioning was an affirmation and expression of support for the ministry of those who would be laboring directly to meet the widows' needs. This process was important. Although the workers were fulfilling their personal sense of mission and calling, the church was also participating in their ministry and was reaching out through them. The commissioning made the workers, the church, and the widows aware that this ministry was part of the mission of the laity as a whole. It was not the work of individuals alone. There was a corporate dimension and awareness to their labor. This was accomplished in part through commissioning.

Emphasis on Function Rather Than Institution (Acts 1:15-26; 13:1-3; 1 Timothy 3:1-13)

The New Testament church maintained practical and functional structures of organization. When, in Acts 1, there was a practical need to replace one of the apostles, the Spirit moved upon the church, and it organized a selection process to meet this need. The need was to find someone to take part in fellowship, ministry, and leadership with the other 11 apostles.

In Acts 13, there was a need for further expansion and evangelism. The Spirit moved upon the people of the church at Antioch, and Paul and Barnabas were selected and sent forth as missionaries.

In 1 Timothy 3:1-13, there was a need for qualified leaders. In this section and others, especially in the Pastoral Epistles, Paul emphasized the practical spiritual qualities required for leadership in the church. There were various levels and functions of leadership, including deacons, elders, and overseers. Each had requirements for service and character.

In each of these examples, the criteria were set by the leadership of the Holy Spirit. The goal was not preservation of an institution. The organization that developed served functional purposes. The changes and processes of administration came about by the Holy Spirit's working in the lives of those involved.

Operated With a Sense of God-centered Mission (Acts 13:1-3)

When the church at Antioch organized its missionary activity, it did so under God-centered direction. The focus of their selection and commissioning of missionaries was not a purely intellectual process. The need to evangelize the Gentile world was evident. However, the emphasis of the record in Acts 13 is on the central direction they received from God.

The work of the laity and pastoral leadership must take into account physical as well as spiritual needs. However, the New Testament clearly records that the first sense of direction that the apostles desired was God-centered. The traditions and philosophies that guided their activities and the work of the church was centered on Christ and not on men (Colossians 2:6-23).

Pastoral Development of Lay Ministry

Establish Priority of God's Action and Will in the Life of the Church

The church must be a discerning body that knows the action and will of God. The church claims that in Christ they live out the will of Christ in the world. The first step in doing this is to discern what that will is.

The ministry and vision of the church must be a God-centered mission. All other goals are secondary. The pastor and leadership must participate with the body in presenting what they perceive to be the action and will of the Lord in the church.

A direct statement needs to be developed also concerning the congregation's perception of God's action and mission in the church. Goals then need to be aligned with that central mission. Further, the organization of the church must be structured according to the church's mission and goals. The ultimate claim of the body is that it operates according to God-centered directives, not a man-made program.

The burden is upon each believer in the church to discern God's action and will in the body. Study of the Word, teaching ministries, worship, song, praise, and all other ministries of the church should enhance the believers' perception and search for the central power and presence of the Lord.

Discerning God's Mission Must Be Lived Out in Discipleship, Love, and Witnessing

The task of establishing the priority of a God-centered mission begins in the life of each believer. The believer must develop skills of personal discipleship. The ministries of the church should equip the laity to study the Word for themselves. Ministries of the body should call individuals to a life of prayer. Each person should be taught the priority of family relationships as an extension of Christian discipleship (Ephesians 5:21—6:4; Colossians 3:17-21). All these areas are means whereby individual believers may discern the will of God for their lives and His acts in their lives and the life of the church.

Love within the community of the church must be fostered by the organization of the church. In other words, the church should organize administrative functions and activities that encourage the members to demonstrate their love for each other through loving actions. The structure of the church should invite communion with God and others within the fellowship of the church. Recognition of the ministry of each person in the body also fosters this kind of love. Love for the body of believers is part of the salvation message of the church (John 13:34-36).

The ministry of the church to the world is an outgrowth of God's work through individuals and of the world's recognition of believers' love for another. This can be diagramed as follows:

Sequence in Ministry

The central priority of God establishes the sequence
of ministry and the order in which personal
discipleship and love within the body of Christ
precedes witness to the world.

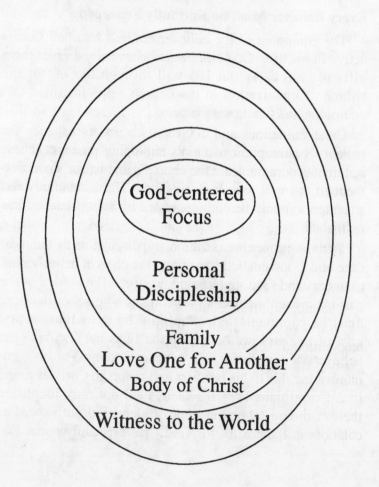

God-centered
Focus

Personal
Discipleship

Family
Love One for Another
Body of Christ
Witness to the World

Having a God-centered focus and mission results in the development of personal discipleship. Personal discipleship results in love for one another. Love for one another results in a witness to the world. If there is no personal discipleship, love for one another will be diminished. If love for one another is diminished, then the church's witness to the world will be ineffective.

Every Believer Must Be Carefully Equipped

The equipping of the believer reminds him that God is active in his life. God empowers believers and gives them gifts to help carry out His will through the life of the church. Organization in the church helps facilitate this equipping and functioning process.

Clear guidelines and doctrinal statements enhance the believer's perception of God's equipping process. These statements communicate the church's and pastor's commitment to the will and work of God. These standards and statements should be communicated by being clarified and published.

Without proper organization and circulation of the message and God-centered mission of the church, believers fail to understand God's equipping process. The burden of the pastor for each member to function as a vessel of the Lord must be communicated. Paul said he shared a common goal of ministry not only with the Lord but also with the believers of the church. An excellent example of his communicating this to his brothers and sisters in Christ is found in 2 Corinthians 6:1-10, where Paul not only identified their common labor but clearly identified with them as colabors in their work for God. He especially noted that

God was working through each of them in the midst of various circumstances—both good and bad—to accomplish His work.

Effective Development of Lay Ministry From the Perspective of the Pastor

The equipping of the body many times comes first through the equipping of its leadership. This is especially true of the pastor. The flock is unprotected and becomes sick and scattered when there is no shepherd with a burden (Matthew 9:35-38). The pastor must first establish the sovereignty of God in his own heart, and humility before God is where this process of equipping begins.

Effective action and perception of the power and presence of God in the church does not depend on external circumstances. It depends much more on the condition of the hearts of the members of the body (Luke 12:1-12). The heart of the pastor must be especially attuned to the Chief Shepherd in order to lead the flock in the right ways (John 17; 1 Peter 5:1-11). The people of God will be shepherded by God regardless of the condition of the human shepherd (Ezekiel 34). Nevertheless, God's intention is for those called to pastoral leadership to lead with a heart committed to God. As a result, ministry flows out of that commitment.

Principles for the Financial Structure of the Church

The Bible offers important insights for the financial ministry of the local church, and the pastor bears the responsibility of communicating these to the body. The pastor is responsible for keeping accurate records and for communicating the financial status of the church to its members. Further, the pastor must exhort each believer to share in the financial ministry of the church.

The congregation must have a voice in setting policies and making plans for the church. Regardless of the size of the congregation, the members are entitled to regular reports of the church's financial status. The needs and resources of congregations vary; nevertheless, each person should feel a sense of responsibility for the church's financial mission. A local church may use a variety of means to accomplish this, including general meetings, the church council, a finance committee, or the church clerk. This process is most effective when it is rooted in a scriptural understanding of the financial ministry of the church.

The Principle of Tithing

Tithing is one of the most significant principles for the financial ministry of the local church. The term *tithe*—both in the Hebrew (*asar*) and the Greek (*dekatee*) essentially means "tenth." In the verb form it carries the meaning "to give a tenth." These terms and their derivatives occur 30 times in the Old Testament and seven times in the New Testament. Four times in the New Testament (Matthew 23:23; Luke 11:42; 18:12; Hebrews 7:5) the term carries the added meaning "to tithe as a debtor."

Tithing is a vital part of our relationship with God. The amount of payment is important but not as important as the relationship. When we do not tithe, we actively detract (*rob*, Malachi 3:8) from what is actually God's. Tithing is directly related to what we receive from God, and tithing is an integral part of God's storehouse (v. 10).

Tithing in Scripture occurred as early as the time of

Abraham. Abraham gave tithe to Melchizedek as an act of adoration and praise to God. God had just used Abraham to defeat the enemy, and God used Melchizedek to pronounce His blessing on Abraham after the victory.

In the Old Testament, reference to *tithe* occurs most often in the Books of the Law, Nehemiah, and 2 Chronicles. The greatest emphasis recorded was during the time of Moses. Tithing was also paid during the time of the monarchy. It was strongly supported by Nehemiah (10:37).

The Book of Malachi also deals with tithing. Malachi issued a strong rebuke for the failure of the people to be faithful in the expression of their love and worship of the Lord through tithing. As a result of their straying from God's ordinances, of which their failure to tithe was a part, God called them to true repentance. The failure to tithe is identified with robbing God (3:7-12). Tithing is seen as an offering to God, not to man. It is also seen as one the prerequisites to God's blessings.

The Principle of Stewardship

Another concept significant for understanding the financial ministry of the church is that of *steward*. Stewardship in both the Old and New Testaments referred to the oversight, management, or distribution of someone else's goods. It did not refer to the proper management of one's own personal goods. The word *steward* also includes these meanings—"commissioner, manager, and guardian." And all these refer to possessions owned by a master or lord.

In the Bible, the concept of stewardship did not include many of those commonly attached to it today. It did not mean "giving" or "acts of service." Stewardship was the administration and oversight of goods and property owned by another. A steward was someone responsible to and under the authority of another (Luke 16:2-4; Acts 26:12; 1 Corinthians 4:1, 2). It was a ministry offered by the saints as a result of the grace of God (1 Peter 4:10, 11). A Christian steward was seen as someone working under God's permission (1 Corinthians 16:7; Hebrews 6:3). It also involved training and tutoring for effectiveness.

Godly stewardship is the management and resourceful utilization of God's possessions. It is a responsibility given by God to His servants, involving His goods. Stewardship is a reflection of one's relationship with God and not just how ably we manage goods, services, and money. It is part of our ministry to God and others.

The concept of stewardship applies to the financial ministry of the church. The possessions of the believer are theirs by the grace of God. In this sense, the management of one's personal resources is seen as a service to God. It is not merely the resourceful use of one's possessions. Acts of stewardship and giving were directed to the Temple in the Old Testament (Malachi 3) and the body of believers in the New Testament (Acts 2:41-47; 4:31—5:11). The same concept of bringing the fruits of God's blessings and resources back to His house still applies today. This is the role of stewardship in the local church.

Giving as Ministry Unto the Lord and the Saints (2 Corinthians 9)

> For as touching the ministering to the saints . . . make up beforehand your bounty, whereof ye had notice before . . . for your liberal distribution unto them" (2 Corinthians 9:1, 5, 13).

Paul here presented a biblical description of the financial ministry of the local congregation. In this chapter, he was writing to a specific local congregation, addressing a specific financial ministry. It is concrete enough, however, to relate to other specific financial issues of a local church today. This chapter is one of the most thorough treatments of financial ministry found in Scripture.

Paul called the financial matters he was dealing with a ministry to the saints (v. 1). It is not just a fiscal matter of balance sheets and equity. The essential goal must be to use financial resources as a ministry to others for the glory of God. The term *ministry* is from the Greek *diakonos*. *Deacon* comes from the same root word. It stresses attention given to the physical needs of others.

Paul was not afraid to talk about the advance preparation that had been made for the church's giving, as is especially evident in verse 5: ". . . that they would go before unto you, and make up beforehand your bounty." In some instances in a local church, spontaneous giving is necessary as unexpected needs arise. However, planned giving is clearly biblical.

Paul emphasized the inner motivation of the person that participates in the financial ministry of the church. In fact, this is emphasized rather than the amount the church was to give. The church in Jerusalem was in need, and Paul was attempting to collect enough to bring them aid. Although nothing is said about the amount expected, great emphasis was placed on the inner condition of the giver. This is especially borne out in these words: "As he purposeth in his heart, so let him give; not grudgingly, or of necessity " (v. 7).

The majority of Paul's address concerning the financial

ministry of the church focused on God's response and involvement. Paul emphasized God's loving response to a "cheerful giver." He stressed that God gives abounding grace to those that give to the financial ministry (v. 10). Paul said the giver should give with an attitude of thanksgiving before God (v. 11). Finally, the climactic conclusion of Paul's theme is that God has given so much already to the believer, especially His "unspeakable gift"—the Lord Jesus Christ (v. 15).

The Importance of Bookkeeping, Reporting, and Accountability

Responsible maintenance of records and reporting of the economic condition of the church enhances the financial ministry of the church. It indicates that the offerings and tithe received by the church are the product of the faithfulness of the people of the body of Christ. Accurate and responsible accounting is an affirmation of godly stewardship. Reporting to the congregation makes the finances of the church the ministry of the entire body. Individual givers are mentioned in Scripture (Acts 4:36—5:11). However, the emphasis is upon the contributions of the body as a whole (Acts 2:41-47; 4:31-35). Maintaining proper accountability to the body is a mark of this emphasis.

The financial ministry of the church is part of the worship of the church. It reflects the continuing strength of the church's relationship to the Lord. Giving is an opportunity to express thanksgiving to God for His gifts to us. Finances are not presented as a method of "buying" the blessings of God. However, God does grant abundant grace to those who give abundantly from the heart and with faithfulness to the financial ministry of the church.

The Pastor and the Worship of the Church

6

There is a strong sense of fellowship between the pastor and congregation during worship. The pastor as a worship leader must bear certain vital concerns. This chapter will investigate some of these concerns.

Pivotal Role of the Pastor: Models of Prophet and Priest

Two important models for worship leadership are presented in Scripture—prophet and priest. In the role of prophet, the worship leader bears the Word of the Lord to the congregation.

Functioning as a prophet, the pastor as worship leader brings the concerns of God before the congregation. These concerns may be expressed as a word, a message, or a burden brought to the people from God through the worship leader. It is prophetic in nature and does not come from human resources.

The other role for worship leadership is priest. The biblical function of the priest was to bring the people to God. The priest expressed the concerns, sins, and offerings of the people to God. In this manner, the pastor as worship leader bears the cares and praise of the body to the heavenly Father. This does not negate the communication and relationship each individual believer has with the Father. Rather, it identifies the special representative function the pastor as worship leader can have. The pastor represents the people before God. Through intercessory prayer, exhortation of the Word, and direct intervention before the Lord, the pastor serves in a priestly role in worship leadership.

The Importance of True Worship: The Failure of Jeroboam

Several examples of worship leadership are found in the kings of Israel and Judah. At times, the kings had opportunities to lead the people of God in worship, praise, and revival. Personal and spiritual factors in their lives especially affected their ability as worship leaders. Particular attention will be given to these factors in this chapter.

> And Jeroboam said in his heart, Now shall the kingdom return to the house of David: If this people go up to do sacrifice in the house of the Lord at Jerusalem, then shall the heart of this people turn again unto their lord, even unto Rehoboam king of Judah, and they shall kill me, and go again to Rehoboam king of Judah. Whereupon the king took counsel, and made two calves of gold, and said unto them, It is too much for you to go up to Jerusalem: behold thy gods, O Israel, which brought thee up out of the land of Egypt (1 Kings 12:26-28).

The story of Jeroboam's worship leadership and the factors that affected it are found in 1 Kings 12:25—13:10.

Jeroboam perverted and distorted the worship of the Lord. He endeavored to mix the worship of God with the worship of the calves in the wilderness of the Exodus (12:26-28). His motivation was selfish gain (12:26, 27). He wanted to manipulate the faithfulness of people. He was willing to sacrifice the true worship of God in order to achieve personal gain.

Jeroboam had been influenced by the counsel of others (12:28, 29, 31-33). His advisors encouraged the distortion of worship. In perverting worship, Jeroboam led the people into sin (12:30). Thus we see the role of the worship leader is of great importance. Many times, people are influenced for good or bad by the person who is leading worship.

God rebuked and judged Jeroboam's corrupt worship leadership. The false altar was broken and Jeroboam's hand "dried up," or lost its strength and ability to move (13:1-6). Jeroboam's misuse of worship affected both the place of worship and himself. This principle is the same today. Eventually, failure to worship in an obedient and pleasing way will result in calamity for both the church and the worship leader.

Approaches to worship vary from congregation to congregation and from culture to culture. However, God discerns the intentions of the heart. He is aware when worship gratifies the flesh and self more than it glorifies Him. He knows when the worship leader is using his role for selfish gain. God demands obedient worship; therefore, a major goal of the pastor as worship leader is to seek the will of the Lord for worship in the congregation and then to be obedient to that will.

Necessity of Personal Submission:
The Arrogance of Uzziah

King Uzziah had been blessed by God. Second Chronicles 26:1-15 gives a detailed description of Uzziah's power, might, and influence. His was one of the most influential kingdoms in Judah's history. But at the pinnacle of his power and influence, Uzziah's pride caused him to abuse the worship of God. He did not personally submit himself before God in worship. As a result of his sin, Uzziah was stricken and never recovered.

King Uzziah became proud and boastful (v. 15). His heart had moved away from the submission he once had had before God (vv. 4, 5). Because of his pride, he went to the altar of the Lord to burn incense (v. 16). He was not permitted access to the altar, much less to burn incense. This was to be done only by the priests. The high priest and 80 other priests confronted Uzziah in the Temple (vv. 17, 18). Scripture records Uzziah's reaction and the response of God's judgment.

> Then Uzziah was wroth, and had a censer in his hand to burn incense: and while he was wroth with the priests, the leprosy even rose up in his forehead before the priests in the house of the Lord, from beside the incense altar. And Azariah the chief priest, and all the priests, looked upon him, and, behold, he was leprous in his forehead, and they thrust him out from thence; yea, himself hasted also to go out, because the Lord had smitten him (2 Chronicles 26:19, 20).

Uzziah had violated the principles of worship leadership. His pride and anger were judged by the Lord. If God endeavors to correct the pastor as worship leader, it may be to reveal some area in his life that needs ministry. Uzziah needed to repent of his pride. This internal process of reflection and confession before the Lord is important. God requires that the leading of worship be in faithful service to his command and will for worship, not in pride and anger.

Leading Others in Worship: The Decisiveness of Hezekiah

Hezekiah decisively led the nation of Israel in worship and renewal at a critical place in their history. They had not worshiped the Lord as they should have. The Temple was in disarray. The neglect of worship had gone on so long the people were used to it. Once Hezekiah perceived the need for renewed worship, he acted quickly and effectively to lead the people back to genuine and fervent worship. It changed the nation.

In 2 Chronicles 29 Hezekiah began his administration by giving priority to worship. He opened the doors of the Temple once again (v. 3). They had been closed because of the neglect of previous leadership and the spiritual condition of the people. Many times a pastor as worship leader faces a congregation that has not worshiped fervently and genuinely for some time. The process of leading people in renewal of worship is similar to the leadership of Hezekiah.

Hezekiah immediately emphasized the importance of purity as preparation for worship (vv. 4, 5; see also Isaiah 1). He started by making certain the worship leaders had been cleansed. Then he proceeded to properly prepare the place of worship.

Worship renewal usually does not begin with a change in the congregation before a change takes place in the heart of the worship leader. Also, the condition and sanctity of the place of worship is often neglected and needs to be renewed before the people respond.

Hezekiah declared the need of the people to return to worship to the Lord (vv. 6-11). He emphasizes several principles:

* The basic problem of sin—*trespassed* (v. 6)

* Lack of priority and willingness—*shut up the doors* (v. 7)

* Did not foster God's presence—*not kept the lamps burning* (v. 7)

* Did not honor the Lord—*not burned incense* (v. 7)

* Did not recognize sinfulness and need—*nor offered burnt offerings* (v. 7)

* God had judged their neglect—*the wrath of the Lord* (v. 8)

In response to the great need he saw, Hezekiah made a personal covenant with the Lord and encouraged his worship leaders to do the same (vv. 10, 11). The impetus for worship begins in the heart of the pastor and the worship leadership, not with the first sounds of music or praise in a worship service. It must begin long before that in heart preparation within the pastor and worship leadership. This is especially true when there has been neglect of genuine worship.

Because of these initial steps taken by Hezekiah, a great revival and renewal of worship took place. The foundation continued to expand in areas of repentance, cleansing, and obedient preparation (vv. 12-27). Devotion and praise were voiced (vv. 28, 29). Gladness was expressed in worship (v. 30). The laity felt the renewal of worship and participated with the leadership in cleansing (30:13, 14). There was cleansing in the midst of the congregation

(v. 17). Hezekiah continued to play a decisive role throughout the worship and renewal process. He prayed for the people (vv. 18-20).

Reformation in Worship Through the Word: Josiah's Burden

King Josiah illustrated the important role of the Word in worship. He used the discovery of the Word of God as an opportunity for leading the people back to godly repentance and worship (2 Kings 22—23). As in the case of Hezekiah, Josiah began by restoring and repairing what had been neglected in worship (22:3-7). In this process, the Word was rediscovered (vv. 8-10). Josiah was moved by the Word and used it as a catalyst for repentance and obedience in worship (22:11-14).

As a result of the discovery of the Word, Josiah initiated certain steps which led to a renewal of worship among the people. These steps included

• Proclamation of the Word (23:1, 2)

• Covenant worship and relationship with God through the Word (23:3)

• Purification through the Word from unclean worship (23:4-20, 24)

• Godly worship as a result of the Word (23:1-3; 2 Chronicles 35).

Josiah's example is a precedent for today. The Word of God can be a catalyst for worship. A heartfelt desire to be obedient to the Word in worship and revival was at the heart of Josiah's worship leadership. The worship leaders around him and the people of the nation were stirred as well. Just as Josiah led with his fervor for the Word, the pastor in worship leadership can also lead a congregation to renewal of genuine worship through exhortation of the Word.

Ministry of the Ordinances of the Church

The Meaning of Liturgy and Worship in the Church

A term which captures the role of service in worship is *liturgy*. It comes from the Greek term, *leitourgos*. It is usually translated "minister." The word or a variation of it occurs 15 times in the New Testament. Various usages include the following:

• One who ministered to the Lord (Acts 13:2)

• Offering as a ministry (Romans 15:27)

• Ministry of Christ as high priest (Hebrews 8:2, 6; 9:21; 10:11)

• The priest ministering in the Temple (Luke 1:23)

• Works and administration as ministry (2 Corinthians 9:12; Philippians 2:17, 30)

• Ministering the gospel (Romans 15:16)

The word had a special, sacred sense. It was used in a variety of ways but always carried the idea of a service unto the Lord. It was not just an act of human service; it was an act of worship. It was used in the Septuagint (Greek translation of the Old Testament) for the work of the Levites in the service of worship. In the New Testament it referred to a special offering of service on behalf of others unto God.

The devout sense of *liturgy* is the type of sacredness necessary in the ministration of the ordinances of the church. The pastor's leadership in the sacraments offers an opportunity to restore a sense of God's presence and power. The service of the sacraments carries the awesome sense of reverence and godly fear required in Scripture. The ordinances are special devout acts done unto God.

Pastoral Ministry and the Sacraments

Lives are shaped by significant events, and in the church these include the celebration of the sacraments. The life of the believer is not shaped by rationalizations or human acts as much as it is by the move of the Spirit in significant experiences of worship. This is the context of the sacraments. They are special times of God's intervention in the church when the Spirit ministers and reminds the Christian of the fundamental aspects of knowing Christ.

Pastoral leadership should make remembrance and celebration of the sacraments in the church a regular part of the life of the church. This does not mean that Communion is served every Sunday, nor does it mean that washing of the saints' feet must be done every month. However, all the ordinances should be a vital, regular, and normal part of the church's activity. They should not be occasional exceptions.

Sacraments served as a central part of Christ's ministry while on earth. He practiced all of them Himself. He instructed the disciples to follow His example. They are part of the Great Commission and recorded as a normal part of the activity of the early church. Christ used the sacraments as special times to communicate truth. They were not merely rituals exercised for Him; they were acts of worship and service unto the Father.

The Theology and Ministry of the Lord's Supper

The Lord's Supper is a communal meal of the church which remembers Christ's work and active presence in the church. The precedent for this type of celebration was in the peace offering of the Old Testament (Leviticus 3:1-17; 7:11-38; 22:21). In the Old Testament celebration, a fellowship meal with the Lord as host was celebrated by each family. Now the Lord is the host through the person of Christ. Christ commanded the disciples to celebrate Communion as an act of remembrance. This remembrance extends to the recognition of His presence in the midst of those worshiping in Communion.

The Lord's Supper is also an offering of thanksgiving unto the Lord. The roots of this celebration of thanksgiving can be found in the Old Testament sacrifice of thanksgiving (Leviticus 7:12-15; 22:29-33; Psalm 107:22; 116:17; Amos 4:5). Communion is a time to express gratefulness for the work of Christ. It is a time to remember and express thanksgiving unto the Lord. It turns the heart of the believer toward thanksgiving in an act of obedient celebration.

The believer identifies with the suffering of the Lord by partaking in Communion. It is becoming part of the generation mentioned in Isaiah 53:8 that declares and remembers the suffering of the Lord. In Isaiah 53 the suffering and sacrifice of the Lord is given in graphic description. The call is given for all those who would participate in the declaration of that work. The Lord's Supper is such a declaration. Further, in Hebrews 13:10-15 the believer is exhorted to go to the Lord who has become the sacrifice for our sins. Communion is a fulfillment of this going forth unto the One who was slain in our behalf.

Finally, the Lord's Supper is a participation in the remembrance of the Passover Meal. Christ was the Lamb slain for the believer, just as the lamb was slain for each household of the Exodus. Communion is a remembrance of the blood sacrifice of the Lord, similar to the blood on the doorposts that guaranteed the protection of the first-born of each participating family. Christ's sacrifice is a delivering and protecting work for the believer. Communion is a celebration akin to the Passover, where the work of God was remembered. Just as Passover was a memorial (Exodus 12:14), so Communion is a remembrance unto the Lord.

Administering the Lord's Supper

The Lord's Supper is an opportunity to involve members of the congregation in a team approach. The preparation of the elements, the overall planning of administration, and the actual service itself can all involve different persons. This team approach is a good reflection of the body-life ministry of the church. Members of the Church and Pastor's Council can be used in order to reflect the leadership of the church in ministry. It can be a time to train others as potential worship leaders.

The primary parts of the preparation phase involve the physical preparation of the cups, plates, and bread. Actual bread, unleavened bread, wafers, or crackers can be used. Plates, trays, and covers specially designed for Communion can be purchased in aluminum, silver, brass, or wood. The color of the Communion set can especially complement a sanctuary. Planning for an adequate amount of cups and bread needs to be carefully done.

Planning the order and arrangement in which the elements will be passed needs to be done ahead of time. Each tray holds approximately 40 cups. Two people should be assigned for every 40 participants. This can be expanded to four, two for the cups and two for the bread plate. Even if there are 600 people participating, the timing of the serving can be gauged according to the amount of time it takes to serve 40 people. Each set of 40 persons will be served simultaneously.

The actual place on the church calendar needs to be given thought. Again, this can be a reflection of the priorities and body-life ministry of the church. The more regular the offering of Communion, the more it will be seen as a natural part of the life of the church. If Communion is offered only occasionally or at the last minute, with little planning or announcement, it will reduce the importance of the event.

The use of wine in Communion is not explicitly given in Scripture. Only "the cup" is mentioned in Matthew 26:26-30 and Luke 22:19, 20. "Fruit of the vine" is mentioned in Matthew 26:29. However, crushed grape juice serves the same intention of representing the brokenness and shed blood of the Lord. In no case does the drink actually become the blood of the Lord.

Several different models can be used in arranging the Lord's Supper. In one model, the elements are placed on a table at the front of the sanctuary and are served at some point in a service, usually at the end, by a team. In another model, a table with 13 chairs is set at the front of the sanctuary. One chair remains empty, representing the presence of the Lord. Persons come in groups and partake of Communion under the direction of the pastor. This model is used for special occasions where there is more time to emphasize families or groups. Another model combines the Lord's Supper with the washing of the saints' feet. It is best to have the Communion service first. This combination is an emphasis of the account in John 13.

The Theology and Ministry of Water Baptism

The authority and commission to baptize can be found in several New Testament passages, especially Matthew 28:19. It was intended by Christ as a part of the ministry of the church. It is a demonstration of the overcoming power of the Lord (Matthew 28:18). Water baptism is a vital part of the evangelistic ministry of the church. It is a significant part of the discipleship and growth of every believer.

Water baptism was not intended to replace repentance and salvation. It serves as a remembrance and visible expression to the church and the world of the work that God has done in an individual. Salvation is a matter of trust in and repentance to the Lord. It is a personal act by which an individual gains access into the kingdom of God. Water baptism, as important as it is, does not replace the necessity of salvation.

Water baptism is an event in which the church participates. It is an expression of personal commitment by the believer. It is also an act of corporate commitment by the church. The believer communicates his commitment to the Lord and the church while the church expresses its commitment to the believer. Water baptism is also an expression of personal and corporate commitment unto God whereby the individual and the church express their commitment together to the Lord.

Water baptism is an external act that expresses the inner

work Christ has already accomplished. For the Jews at the time of Christ, baptism was merely an affirmation of one's religious affiliation. John the Baptist and then Jesus transformed the concept to include repentance and newness of life. It is a declaration of a personal covenant with God. A person signifies his death and burial to sin as he is lowered into the water. He illustrates newness of life and commitment to Christ as he is raised from the water.

Administering Water Baptism

Preparation for the service of water baptism is important. Classes for baptismal candidates are sometimes conducted. These can be as few as one or two sessions. An orientation for candidates advising them of the details of the service helps make the experience more meaningful.

The orientation time needs to cover the essential scriptural reasons for baptism. The meaning of baptism should be communicated. Especially important is the testimony that is given to others. In fact, many times it is effective to give the candidate an opportunity to give an actual testimony to the congregation before baptism.

Baptism can be integrated with the regular program and services of the church. It also can be seen as an extension of the outreach and evangelism ministries of the church. If a candidate is a participant in a particular ministry in the church or if he was won to the Lord in a particular ministry, those ministries can be highlighted during the baptism. If a ministerial staff member was responsible for leading the person to the Lord or has been working especially close in the discipleship process of the individual, that person might be given the privilege of administering baptism.

In the actual baptismal formula (spoken when baptizing the person) some of the points to stress may include the following:

• Identification of the meaning of baptism (obedience, death, burial, newness of life)

• Recognition of various attributes of God (care, love, etc.)

• Affirmation of the Trinity in baptism (Father, Son, and Holy Ghost)

• Baptism is on the basis of the candidate's confession of faith in the Lord Jesus Christ.

When baptizing an individual it is important to make sure it is done properly. The physical care of the candidate needs to be taken into account. As much as possible, the temperature of the water needs to be appropriate. If the baptism is in an outdoor stream, river, pool, or canal, the area needs to be checked ahead of time for safety.

The baptismal candidate should hold a wrist with one hand and hold his nose with the other hand while allowing the cup of the hand to cover his mouth. The minister should place his hand on the upper back of the candidate to support him as he goes into the water. At the actual moment of immersion, the individual can be gently led into leaning back with the supporting hand of the minister behind him. After the candidate is immersed, the minister can raise him, using the arm supporting the individual's back. It is also suggested that the minister use his bent legs as leverage to lift the candidate.

The Theology and Ministry of Washing the Saints' Feet

Washing the saints' feet is an ordinance of the church.

It has been questioned by many in modern church history. However, Christ practiced and commanded this observance. Essentially, it is an act of worship unto the Lord which emphasizes humility of service unto one another and the Lord. It was a regular practice of the early church. Christ set the standard for the practice when He washed the disciples' feet the night of the Lord's Supper.

The criteria for observing the Lord's Supper, water baptism, and washing the saints' feet as ordinances of the church are all the same. They were all practiced by Christ. They were all commanded of Christ to be followed. Finally, they were all recorded as being practiced by the early church.

The record of the washing of the saints' feet as a regular practice in the early church is found in the list of qualifications for a worthy widow (1 Timothy 5:10). It was an act of worship, not hospitality, because when hospitality was intended, it was explicitly so named (Romans 12:13; 1 Timothy 3:2; Titus 1:8; 1 Peter 4:9).

The primary text for the teaching of the washing of the saints' feet is found in John 13:1-20. The washing of the disciples' feet was such a vital part of the events of Christ's last night with them that John gave it major attention. In fact, John highlighted this event and only briefly mentioned the Lord's Supper (vv. 13:2-4). It was a special illustration of Christ's humility before the one who would betray Him. It was also the foundation for the new commandment of love He gave to the disciples (vv. 31-35).

Christ emphasized the obligation the disciples had to follow His example. He said, "Ye also ought to wash one another's feet" (v. 14). *Ought* was a command. It carried the idea of continuing obligation, not a onetime act. Carrying out this act of worship and humble service is a fulfillment of this command and obligation.

In verse 15, He said, "For I have given you an example." His intention was that they should follow His example continually. Christ was referring to the actual event of washing the saints' feet, not to a mere principle or general set of actions.

Washing of the feet was not just an old Jewish custom. They were in the habit of washing their own feet (Genesis 18:4; 19:2). But Christ was introducing a new practice. He was not reenacting a custom or merely fulfilling a routine domestic function. It was an act of worship and service unto God the Father.

Christ had specific purposes and results in mind when He washed the disciples' feet. The experience was to result in happiness (John 13:17). It was for the spiritual cleansing of the disciples (v. 18). It was a recognition of God's authority as Master over them (vv. 13-16). The disciples would eventually remind themselves of Christ's worship and humility. Further, they would carry out the same acts themselves as His followers.

Kenneth Wuest's translation of John 13:14, 15 is a fitting summary of the principles inherent in the washing of the saints' feet: "Since thererefore I, the Lord and the Teacher, washed your feet, you also have a moral obligation to be washing one another's feet, for I gave to you an example that just as I did to you, you also should be doing."

Administering the Washing of the Saints' Feet

This ordinance is not usually practiced as much as the other ordinances. However, it needs to be practiced regularly. It does require a greater amount of preparation, but the command of the Lord is as clear with this ordinance as it is with the others. Therefore, washing the saints' feet needs to be seen as part of the regular life of the church and not as an occasional exception.

Care must be given in preparation of the service to let the congregation understand the importance of this ordinance. This is especially true if a church has not practiced it in some time. Teaching on the ordinance a few services in advance will be very helpful. Advance announcement is important because some members of the congregation may not be familiar with the ordinance.

Preparation for the washing of the saints' feet includes deciding where and how to integrate it in the worship service. It is usually best to have the ordinance at the end of a service. Many times a brief intermission or time of worship is conducted before the ordinance is begun to allow time for preparation of rooms, basins, and towels.

A suggested format for the ordinance is to have rooms to the side of the sanctuary prepared for the washing of feet. The congregation is divided into groups, meeting in separate rooms. One major purpose for this division is lack of sufficient space for the basins and administration of the ordinance. At times, the sanctuary may be used for one group. In each room, a set number of basins are prepared in a row. Each basin is set in front of a chair. Individuals select another person with whom to administer the ordinance. One person sits on the chair while the other person washes his feet.

When individuals enter the room there is usually a brief time of dividing into pairs, finding chairs, and removing shoes, socks, or stockings. The water may or may not be already poured into the basins. Towels may be furnished by the church, or an announcement can be made in advance for everyone to bring a towel. A team of individuals is necessary to prepare the basins in the rooms, arrange the chairs, and place the towels. Also, they can assist in changing the water in the basins. Buckets with fresh water are frequently stationed in each room.

Each pair of individuals can work in the following manner. One person sits in the chair. The other person leans down, placing the towel in his lap or at the side. Each foot is placed in the basin of water separately and with cupped hands the person kneeling washes it. The procedure is repeated with the other foot.

In each room, a leader can provide instructions. The leader can also read from John 13:4-17, minister briefly about the ordinance, and lead in prayer. The pattern of the Lord found in verses 4, 5 and 12 can be emphasized:

• Preparation of garments ("laid aside his garments")

• Use of towel ("took a towel," "wipe them with the towel")

• Kneeling, preparing to wash feet ("girded himself")

• Use of the basin and washing of the feet ("he poureth water into a bason, and began to wash the disciples' feet")

• Putting shoes back on and entering into worship ("after he had washed their feet, and had taken his garments, and was set down again . . .").

The group can take time for praise and worship as each pair finishes. Since other pairs may be waiting if there are not enough basins, the leader may want to wait and lead the entire group in prayer and praise. Or each group can return to the sanctuary for a time of worship after the ordinance is completed. At times the service may be considered dismissed when each group is finished.

Foot washing requires a greater amount of physical preparation ahead of time than the other ordinances. For this reason, it may not be practical to practice the ordinance as often as the others. However, its importance must not be minimized. In large congregations, it might be more logistically possible to have foot washing at separate times or within different departments of the church. In any case, it is a very meaningful and necessary ordinance that reminds the body of believers of the necessity of humble service to one another and worship unto the Lord.

The Ministry of the Word Through Preaching and Teaching

7

The principles upon which the preacher feels a sermon is based directs his perception and interpretation of preaching. Whether the sermon in the mind and heart of the preacher is an exposition of ideas or an act of stewardship of the things of God will determine the course and effect of the message. Everyone who preaches has a certain set of assumptions about preaching. The theological assumptions a minister makes about preaching greatly affect the sermon. The purpose of this chapter is to explore some biblical perspectives about preaching.

The Event of the Word

How then shall they call on him in whom they have not believed? and how shall they believe in him of whom they have not heard? and how shall they hear without a preacher? And how shall they preach, except they be sent? as it is written, How beautiful are the feet of them that preach the gospel of peace, and bring glad tidings of good things! (Romans 10:14, 15).

Preaching is an event in which the Word is sent through a preacher. The term *preacher* in the text above is translated from the Greek term *kerussontos*. The word in this context means "one who continually proclaims." The ancient function of such a person was to simply announce an official message. The proclamation was an event where a message was brought to a group of people. The message was already established, and the person making the announcement was given the authority to declare that message.

The pastor is not called to convey his own message. His responsibility is to declare the message Christ has provided. Belief in the hearts of men and women does not begin with a message of human origin, though it may include the testimony and participation of the human vessel proclaiming the Word. However, the preacher is essentially called to proclaim a message originated by Christ himself.

The focus of Romans 10:14, 15 begins with the origination and commissioning of the message. Paul asked, "And how shall they preach, except they be sent?" The preacher has been sent. This means that the message begins with the Lord and that the preacher has been sent to bear the message the Lord has given.

This implies that the first question the preacher must ask is not "What can I say to this congregation?" Rather, the first question the preacher must ask is "What is God saying through His Word to this congregation?" The preacher must be profoundly aware of the influence and power of the Lord in the preparation and delivery of the sermon. Since the message should originate with the Lord, this awareness is the first priority of the preacher. This is an event of awareness and experience of God's power and presence. The sermon is not the mere presentation of the thoughts of an individual.

The Fear of the Lord and the Sermon

The awesome sense of God's directing and sending power and presence is fostered by what Scripture calls "the fear of the Lord." The fear of the Lord places the preacher in touch with the sovereign action of God in the midst of His people. Also, it brings the awareness of God in contrast to resistance that may come in the midst of the proclamation of the Word.

In Ezekiel 2:1—3:11, God instructed Ezekiel to persevere in proclaiming the Word of the Lord. The Word of the Lord was to be the basis of the message. Ezekiel was not to emphasize his own words or the words of others. He was to deliver the message in such a way that it would be known as the Word of the Lord. This was especially true because the opposition described in this passage was great. It graphically illustrates the looks, reactions, and responses of the people to the message. They were not positive or responsive. Nonetheless, Ezekiel could still preach because he was proclaiming a message that originated with God.

God graphically described the resistance that Ezekiel would encounter. The people would be rebellious, transgressors, impudent, and stiffhearted (2:3, 4). God warned Ezekiel that they were supposed to respond but they would not (3:5-7).

God told Ezekiel the key to facing the people was the power of God within him. God promised Ezekiel He would work within him and exhorted him not to fear nor be dismayed (v. 9). He would strengthen him so that he would be strong enough to face the people (v. 8).

God especially exhorted Ezekiel to guard his own heart and not be rebellious himself. The tragic reality is that if a pastor does not overcome the resistance of individuals to his pulpit ministry by relying upon the work of God within him, he will become like the very people who are resisting him. The pastor who depends upon human instrumentality rather than the power of God to overcome rebellion and resistance to the gospel will himself become rebellious and distant from God (see 2:8; 3:10).

Confidence in the work and presence of the Lord is taught by Jesus in Luke 11:39—12:12. In that passage, Jesus and the disciples were threatened by the Pharisees and the multitude. In the midst of the opposition, He taught the disciples concerning the fear of the Lord. Essentially, He told them that they were not to fear the crowd but the Lord: "And I say unto you my friends, Be not afraid of them that kill the body, and after that have no more that they can do. But I will forewarn you whom ye shall fear: Fear him, which after he hath killed hath power to cast into hell; yea, I say unto you, Fear him" (12:4, 5).

Jesus was preparing the disciples for the time when they would encounter opposition to their preaching. The Holy Spirit would give them the words to speak if they were abiding in the fear of the Lord (12:11, 12). This does not mean that preparation is not needed in preaching. Sermons must be adequately and properly prepared. Neither is this advocating the elimination of notes or reading from a manuscript. Rather, this passage instructs the preacher that the source of his message does not come from himself. Neither should the message come in fearful reaction to how people may or may not respond to a message or resist the message. Jesus' teaching was that the fear of the Lord in preparation for ministry must be greater than our fear of man.

The Preached Word Is for People

The preached Word is not for the purpose of elaborating on abstractions or ideologies. It is the revelation of the power and presence of God himself to and for people. God does not work in behalf of ideologies. Christ did not die for abstractions. Neither should the sermon merely expound ideas. The Word of God is directed to people; therefore, the sermon should be directed to people. It is not the mere transmission of information. It is God speaking to people through the Word.

The Power of the Word Itself Upon the Congregation

The preacher must be certain that the Word in and of itself moves with power upon the congregation. The preacher participates in this process. However, the Word has power in and of itself which comes from the power and presence of God. Before the preacher even reads his text, the Word is alive with the power of God. The mistake is to think that the Word needs the preacher. The very opposite is true—the preacher needs the Word.

The power of the Word is always there. The power of the Word does not originate in human ability. Humans can distract others from the power of the Word and cause them to miss the application of the power of the Word. The preacher must deliver the Word with the certainty that its power is always active, and he must be careful not to do anything that would distract from that power.

The Sermon Is the Proclamation of the Word of God

The sermon should always point to the Word and God's action in the Word. God is active in the midst of the congregation through the Word and the preaching of the Word. This should be the focus and proclamation of the preacher. The sermon should come from, and point toward, the Word. The text of the sermon and God's action should form the organization of the sermon.

Focusing and proclaiming the Word is emphasized when the congregation is invited and encouraged to seek the Word of God for themselves during the message. They should be encouraged to listen to the preacher and open their Bibles to receive from the Word. The preacher should refer to the text often in order to place focus upon the Word.

Nothing the preacher does should shift attention from God's action through the Word. Gestures and illustrations are appropriate only as long as they place focus on the Word. If they are merely subjective or draw attention toward oneself and not the Word, they should not be used. God should always be seen as being larger than the sermon. The Word and its present power should be larger than the preacher.

Preaching the Word and the Worship of the Church

Various Parts of the Worship of the Church

In this section the worship aspects of the local church

will be surveyed and the role of preaching in the worship service will be presented.

In Ephesians 5:18-20 worship was the first aspect of the Spirit-filled life emphasized by Paul. Paul presented three main aspects of worship—*speaking* to one another in public worship, *singing* within oneself in private worship, and *giving thanks* to God: "Speaking to yourselves in psalms and hymns and spiritual songs, singing and making melody in your heart to the Lord; giving thanks always for all things unto God and the Father in the name of our Lord Jesus Christ" (vv. 19, 20).

Speaking referred to an act of declaration to one another in public worship. Worship is something done to honor God. However, Paul further indicated that believers in worship could exhort one another as well. This could be done through the use of "psalms and hymns and spiritual songs" (v. 19). Psalms were songs with musical accompaniment. *Hymns* highlighted the sacred beauty and praise a song of worship could offer unto God. *Songs* were those known for lyric and poetic beauty.

The second aspect of worship is *singing* within oneself for private worship. This, along with "making melody in your heart" (v. 19), was a reference to personal worship. Paul encouraged that in addition to worshiping with others, worship could also be deeply personal—both while in a crowd and when alone.

The third aspect of worship is *giving thanks* to God. The grammar of the Greek text indicates that the giving of thanks is to be a continual part of the believer's life—an attitude that affects the believer's level of gratefulness.

The Function of Preaching

The function of preaching in the worship of the church is in large part to give perspective and place for the ministry of the Word of God. The various aspects of worship described above have various emphases. Praise and adoration are highlighted by song and the cry of the heart unto God. Edifying one another offers praise unto the Lord as the congregation worships God together. And the acts of thanksgiving through tithes, offerings, and other themes highlighted in worship give praise unto God.

Into the midst of these, preaching focuses the attention of the people on the Word of the Lord. Preaching brings the attention of the people to the Word of God in a way that very few, if any, of the other aspects of worship do. This is the distinctive contribution of the sermon.

In worship, preaching becomes the communication of God to man through His divine Word. The preached Word sheds divine light on the other aspects of worship so that they gain clearer focus and are directed toward God in a greater way. Preaching brings the Word to bear upon the life and worship of the church.

Going Beyond Human Instrumentality

The preached Word is greater than any human instrumentality. The worship of the congregation and even the preacher must not supersede the power and presence of the Word of God. Without the Word of God, all else is subject to be interpreted as just human activity and displays of human giftedness. This is not to say that a sermon is required in every service. But it does imply that the Word should be used in every service to give inspiration, illumination, and interpretation. Further, the power of the Word should be presented both in worship and in the message in such a way that the Word's power is evident.

The authority of the preached Word is God's authority, regardless of human resistance. Sometimes this resistance comes during worship or even during the sermon. Nevertheless, the preacher must seek the authority of the Word rather than his own authority.

The temptation is to rely upon human instrumentality for worship and preaching. The ministry of Christ, as Christ preached and as the church bears the Word of the Lord today, is not human in authority or origin. This is the point Jesus made when He was confronted by the Pharisees (Matthew 21:23-46). They asked about the authority of His ministry. Jesus responded by declaring that God works through men, initiating a process that is not of this earth but of heaven. He used John the Baptist's ministry as an example (vv. 23-27). He referred to His own ministry as being of "the Lord's doing" (v. 42). The ministry of the preached Word in the context of worship is not of human instrumentality but of the Lord's action in the midst of His people.

The Teaching Ministry of Pastor and Church

The Goal of the Teaching Ministry of the Church

Every ministry event has the potential for teaching. In the auditorium, the classroom, the fellowship hall, the hallway of the church, or an office, there is opportunity for teaching. The principles of Christ penetrate all of life. An individual does not just live in a classroom. Jesus intended that the classroom of His teachings include all of life. He taught the disciples wherever He went. He taught them on the roadside, in houses, in the countryside, in the garden, at supper, in the Temple court, and in the marketplace. This attitude should permeate the pastor and those involved in the teaching ministry of the church.

The teaching ministry of the church must integrate learning into daily living. The curriculum must be practical and always apply to life. Ivory-tower principles, which are good only for philosophic reflection, must be transformed to apply to living. Christ's gospel is not an ideological masterpiece; it is the key to how we should live before God.

Another goal of the teaching ministry of the church should include an understanding of the "command" aspect of the teachings of Scripture. This principle can be seen in the Great Commission (Matthew 28:20. Christ said to "observe all things" that He had "commanded." Christ intended that His teachings be obeyed as much as they were to be learned. The teachings of Jesus do not just inform the intelligence of an individual, they also are constantly confronting a person to obey.

The word *command* in this passage is translated from the Greek term *entellomai*, which means "to enjoin, to charge." It was a judicial term that called a person to be obedient to a particular injunction. The term was not intended merely for reflection or stimulation of intellect. In the same way the teachings of a church should be designed to impact the lives of parishioners, not just their intellects.

Developing a Network of Teaching Ministry

The teaching leadership of a local church should network with others. Networking is a reflection of the body life of the church. It also demonstrates dependency upon the Word of God, His presence, and His power. Such inter-dependence in teaching guards against the teaching of one particular individual becoming predominant. Teachers can be very influential. Their influence should be used to glorify God rather than to highlight personal abilities.

The most critical network of teaching ministry is with the family. The family is part of the teaching ministry of the church. It is where the principles taught in the life of the church can be affirmed. The home can build upon the foundation established in the teaching ministry of the church. Also, the church can build upon the teaching ministry of the family.

The most influential and significant of all teaching contexts is the home. The relationships that hold the greatest meaning for a person are those between spouses and between parents and children. This calls the church to an emphasis upon parent-child and husband-wife relationships. In these contexts of great significance and meaning, godly teachings must be integrated. Before doctrines and teachings are applied to any other context or life issue, they must be applied to these relationships. At critical times, Paul applied what he taught first to the context of home relationships (Ephesians 5:22—6:4; Colossians 3:18-21; 2 Timothy 1:5; 3:15). The church should do no less today.

Another network concept is the network of individual learners. The curriculum and concepts communicated by the teaching ministry of a local church and pastor are of no effect if they are not directed toward the equipping of the individual believer. The teaching environment of the local church should be designed so that the individual believer is challenged to personally study the Word. This was the spirit of the church at Berea, and it reaped a great harvest (Acts 17:10-12).

The Teaching Ministry of Worship

The worship context of the church can also be developed as a teaching context. When the teachings of the Word are applied in the context of worship, they can be applied in faith and not just intellect. The believer should be encouraged to take what he has learned and apply it in adoration and praise. Worship can be used to give eternal meaning and significance to what has been learned.

The sermon also can be a teaching tool. The pastor can model both teaching and learning while preaching. Examples of the principles the church teaches can be emphasized in the sermon. The believer can be challenged to become a learner as well as a listener during the sermon. Actively engaging the listeners by asking them to look at the passages of Scripture can encourage learning. The learning function during the sermon helps the believer to apply the content to his intellect as well as to his spirit.

Special events in the life and worship of the church provide teaching and learning opportunities. The Lord's Supper can be used as a time to remember and rekindle the work of Christ. Baptism can emphasize the principles of commitment and faithfulness to Christ. Washing the saints' feet can be used to highlight fellowship and humble service to one another. Weddings, dedications, special holidays, and other events also offer teaching opportunities.

The way in which the worship service is conducted is a teaching tool. The time allocated to various parts of the service, comments made during and in between parts of the service, and what may be omitted in worship all teach the congregation something. In a sense, the worship context of the church is the time when the largest class is present to learn. The worship service provides the largest potential for teaching and learning.

Awareness of the Use of Doctrine for Teaching

The pastor is a teacher. A central part of Jesus' ministry was His teachings. As He shepherded the disciples and those around Him, He was teaching. The teachings of Jesus formed the guide for His followers. Jesus taught them by example, by action, and by instruction. All these formed His teachings, which evolved into what the church calls doctrine today. The pastor is involved in the same process, constantly teaching and implementing doctrine into the parishioners' lives.

The doctrines of the church are part of the teaching process. Doctrine is used to guide the body of Christ. The early church developed the apostles' doctrine in order to set standards and guidance. The concept of doctrine has its roots in teaching. The Greek term for *doctrine* (*didache*), which is the same as for *teaching*, implies that the process of doctrine is a teaching process.

Doctrine is not an abstraction or ideology but a teaching communicated to others. The goal of doctrine is not to become a philosophical masterpiece, preserved for its own sake. The true goal of doctrine is to become a teaching and guiding tool for the believer. Doctrines are to edify and equip the believer.

The foundational doctrines of the church are the teachings of the Lord and the apostles. The church continues these doctrines, using them in the same way they were used in the New Testament. They are for building up the body, not simply to identify a body of people. The early church was very concerned that it carry out the same practice and faith followed by others before them who followed the Lord. To assure this, they used the teaching/doctrine process.

A number of godly and ungodly examples of this process of doctrine and teaching are found in the New Testament. Jesus used this process (Matthew 7:28). Paul and others used this process in continuing their Christian faith (Romans 6:17). The apostles' process of teaching was identified as doctrine to be followed (Acts 2:42). Ungodly teachers established unrighteous doctrines through this process. These included Balaam (Revelation 2:14), Nicolaitans (v. 15), and Jezebel (vv. 20, 24).

Implications of Changes in Behavior and Belief

The teaching ministry of the church is important because it affects the behavior of the believer. If the pastor and the church fail to teach, there will be a failure to develop inner principles of faith and spiritual maturity. The behavior of the believer is changed through a process of teaching and discipling. If the pastor and church fail in the teaching ministry of the church, it will be reflected in behavior.

The condition of the heart of an individual affects behavior. In a study of 121 undergraduates at the University of California in 1982, Speckart and Bentler verified that current attitude determined intention more than past behavior. Religious behavior was considered as a major variable. Students were found to act upon attitudes rather than upon the basis of previous behavior (Speckart and Bentler). Fishbein and Ajzen established a model which demonstrated that "behavior is predicated on intention, intention is predicated on attitudes, and attitudes are predicated on beliefs" (Ewald and Roberts). This means a person acts because of the inner development of beliefs. One of the primary areas of the church responsible for developing the maturity of the heart is the teaching ministry of the church. The teaching ministry affects the behavior of those in the church as much as or more than most other ministries.

The teaching ministry of the pastor must encourage growth in Christ by the individual and the community of believers. The pastor's teaching must guide people in the transformation of their character and spiritual lives (Romans 12:1, 2). The pastor must be sensitive to the dynamics of relationships. Morality is formed in the context of community. The instructional task includes the development of a language of faith and use of the language of Scripture. Teaching must be centered around God and His work among His people. God is active in the church, and He has continually used teaching to make His people aware of His presence. The pastor should endeavor to make his teaching ministry a part of God's teaching process.

The Evangelistic Ministry of Pastor and Church

8

The activity, life, and ministries of the local church are perceived and experienced differently by unbelievers than they are by members. Unbelievers do not perceive the church in faith. They see the church as a religious organization, a sociological phenomenon. Though the unbeliever may attach great moral or sentimental value to the church, he does not experience the dynamic power of the Spirit as do members of the body of Christ.

The unbeliever is not a participant in the church, only an observer, though the unbeliever may be present in the church, even participating in the activities of the church. However, until a heartfelt change—an experience of salvation—occurs, the unbeliever will not experience the life of the church in the same way as a Christian. Salvation makes a difference in a person's perception and experience of the church.

The Evangelistic Ministry of the Church

The evangelistic activities of the church must clarify

what is distinctive about the church in comparison to other organizations in the world. The church is different because of Christ. The Spirit of the Lord moves within the church and upon its members. The church is committed to the proclamation of the Word of God. The priorities of the church are dictated by God's will and sovereign action. Without these distinctions being made clear by the body of believers, there will be no effective message to bring to the world. The church is not the message; Christ is. However, Christ uses the church and the members of the body of Christ to represent and transmit the gospel. If the church loses sight of its identity, it will lose its message to the lost.

God is moving upon the earth to accomplish His will. The ministries of the church must equip its members to fulfill the purposes of God upon this earth. The body of Christ is dedicated to the glory of God and the fulfillment of the will of God. If the members of the body are not equipped to perceive and do the will of the Father, they will miss the evangelistic harvest field. The activities of the church have many purposes. However, they must all be directed toward accomplishing the will of the heavenly Father, thereby sending His message to the lost.

The will of God on the earth is to win the lost. Whether the Father is building up the believer, bringing blessings to the church, equipping the body to worship Him, or moving in the midst of any number of ministries in the church, His purpose is the same. The ultimate will of God is for humanity and the church to be redeemed and reconciled unto Himself.

The will of the Father was the focus of Jesus' ministry in winning the lost. This focus was especially illustrated in John 4. After declaring the good news to the woman at the well, Jesus clarified to His disciples that He was fulfilling the will of His heavenly Father: "My meat is to do the will of him that sent me, and to finish his work. Say not ye, There are yet four months, and then cometh harvest? behold, I say unto you, Lift up your eyes, and look on the fields; for they are white already to harvest" (vv. 34, 35).

Jesus' purpose was to draw men into His fold (John 10:15-17). This is the will of the heavenly Father. Jesus' ministry involved many aspects, but they all were directed toward ultimately winning the lost (Luke 19:10). The goals and ministries of the church must be the same as Christ's. The various ministries of the local church ultimately should point toward evangelizing and winning the lost. The mission of the church is to bring the lost into the fold.

The disciples who were with Jesus in Samaria failed to see the will of the Father for evangelism. They were concerned with their own questions instead of the woman in need (John 4:27). The disciples were overly concerned with their own personal needs and wants (vv. 31, 33). Jesus had sent them into the city to reap the evangelistic harvest (v. 38). But they failed to see the will of the Father as Jesus did (vv. 32, 34-38). The need in the city was so great that Jesus had to take two days to minister to the people (v. 40). The disciples failed to see the will of the Father for evangelism because of their self-centered focus, so they walked through the village of Sychar without even seeing its need.

The church today must focus all its ministries upon the will of the Father. This does not mean that every ministry of a local church is evangelistic. It does not mean that evangelism is the only ministry of the church. However, it does mean that the ministries of the church must be sensitive to the will of the Father for redeeming and reconciling the lost. This will help maintain the focus of the church upon the will of the Father for evangelism. The alternative for a local church is to focus only upon itself. The result will be continued insensitivity to the needs of the lost. Just as the disciples walked through Sychar and did not see hungry souls, the church will simply exist for itself in a community and not see those dying around it.

The Essential Catalyst of Repentance Must Be Recognized in the Local Church

Repentance is important because it is the point at which someone begins to enter into the family of God. The disbelief of the unbeliever is turned toward belief with confession and repentance. Whatever the condition of someone who is lost, if he will repent and believe, he will be saved (1 John 1:9).

Repent comes from the Greek term *metanoeo*, which means "to think differently." It emphasizes a change in mind and intention. A person's repentance means a change in intention and will about living. The behavior of the person changes.

The term *repentance*, in its various forms, occurs 64 times in the New Testament. It was the cry of John the Baptist in the wilderness (Matthew 3:2). Repentance was the message of Jesus' preaching (4:17). The lack of repentance was the reason for God's judgment (11:20, 21). Repentance was the center of the disciples' preaching (Mark 6:12). Repentance was the emphasis of the message at Pentecost and continued to be the message of the early church (Acts 2:38; 3:19; 8:22). The message of repentance is central to the activity and evangelistic mission of the church.

The church must be known as a community of those who have repented. If the church resists the priority of repentance, the world will not see evidence of humble submission. If the world sees only the boldness and power of the church but not the cry of repentance, then the sinner will not seek repentance. If the world sees only the glory and splendor of the church and not a lifestyle of repentance before God, the sinner will not know how to approach the sacrifice of the Lord. If the world sees only the success and blessings of the church and not the call to repentance, the sinner will not know the power of repentant surrender to the Lord.

The Work of Evangelism Must Be a Recognition of God's Work

God is continually drawing the world unto Himself. The Holy Spirit works to convict hearts and draw individuals to repentance. God calls the believer to be involved in the winning and discipling of the lost. God transforms lives so that they may become witnesses of Him. God sends forth His followers with His power so that they may convert others.

The church must recognize God's work, not the work of man, as the stimulus for evangelism. The world is not won to Christ because of the evangelistic efforts of men. The lost are drawn to repentance by the work of the Holy Spirit. Human involvement in evangelism must be seen as cooperation with what God is already doing to win the lost. The work of men in evangelism does not make repentance possible.

This does not mean that believers are to do nothing

while God does the work of evangelism. Rather, it means that the Christian's evangelistic work is transformed. The believer must work to win the lost. However, it is not mere human action. It is ministry which is called and empowered by God.

The transformation and empowerment of the believer to win the lost can be illustrated by several texts. The first is the paradigm of the Great Commission. There had been a conspiracy to distort the message about the empty tomb (Matthew 27:62-66; 28:11-15). Thus, some doubted the resurrection and the power of Christ (28:17). Christ responded by declaring that He possessed overcoming power. Further, He exhorted the disciples to win and disciple the nations (28:18-20). The basis of their ability to evangelize the lost was the power of Jesus, not their own power or ability. Likewise, the evangelistic ministry of the local church does not stem from the abilities of men but the empowerment they receive from Christ.

This same principle was evident in the prophets. Isaiah was able to prophesy only because God had empowered him with the coal from the altar (Isaiah 6:6-10). Amos was able to declare the Word of the Lord to the religious authorities and the king of Israel only because God had first given him the message. The message and ability to prophecy did not come from Amos.

The principles and parallels between these passages and the evangelistic ministry of the church today can be illustrated as follows:

Text	Elements of Mission
ISAIAH 6:9	
"Go"	Commission
"Tell"	Declaration
"This people"	People in need
AMOS 7:14, 15	
"Go"	Commission
"Prophesy"	Declaration
"Unto my people Israel"	People in need
MATTHEW 28:18-20	
"Go"	Commission
"Teach" (and baptize)	Declaration
"All nations"	People in need

In each of these texts, the mission of the prophet or the church started with the commission and work of God. It did not begin with the work of the prophet or believer. Neither did it begin with the needs of the people. Evangelism requires the hard work of believers. However, the church and pastor must recognize that the work of evangelism begins with God. The needs of people are met through evangelism. However, the believer must see that evangelism begins with God's commission and power.

The Pastor as Evangelist

The Biblical Basis of the Pastor as Evangelist

Earlier chapters in this book investigated the Old and New Testament perspectives of pastoring. The primary text for the Old Testament was Ezekiel 34. The primary text in the New Testament was John 10. Both of these list evangelism as a major part of shepherding.

In Ezekiel 34 the shepherd is seen doing evangelism. The most direct reference to evangelism is in verse 16: "I will seek that which was lost." The themes of reconciliation and rescue also apply to evangelism. Reconciliation is in verse 16: "And bring again that which was driven away." Rescue is seen in two places, verses 12 and 13. "So will I . . . deliver them out of all places where they have been scattered in the cloudy and dark day. And I will bring them out from the people." This passage helps us to understand how a shepherd is involved in evangelism.

The central task of the shepherd as evangelist is to "seek that which was lost" (v. 16). The Hebrew term for *seek* is *baqash*, which means "to search for diligently with the intention of obtaining." *Lost* (Hebrew, *abad*) means "to be astray and in peril." This implies that the shepherd diligently works to seek out those who are in peril. The shepherd seeks out those who are lost without Christ and in spiritual danger. The evangelistic task of the shepherd takes him to those who have strayed from the fold.

Also in John 10 the shepherd is seen doing the work of evangelism. Evangelism is clearly seen in John 9, and it sets the context for John 10. Evangelism is evident in Christ's burden for "other sheep" (10: 16). Belief is strongly emphasized in John 10. The sheep recognize the shepherd because they believe in Him.

Aspects of Pastoral Function as Related to the Ministry of Evangelism

The pastor must blend pastoral action with the evangelistic mandate. In counseling, preaching, organizing, promoting, visiting the sick, or in any of the other ministries of a pastor, his goal to seek and search for the lost remains. It is the ultimate goal. This is the common denominator of the pastor who fulfills the Great Commission (Matthew 28:18-20).

Paul's ministry serves as a paradigm for the blending of many ministries under the ultimate goal of winning the lost. As church organizer and planter, Paul was concerned for souls. As he developed disciples for Christ in congregations, Paul was ultimately concerned with the redemption of the unsaved. Paul's goal was to preserve those he had shepherded in order to be able to present them to God as redeemed and perfect in Christ (Ephesians 5:27; Colossians 1:22, 28). The eventual goal was evangelistic—that they would not be lost but saved.

Serving as Model, Organizer, and Teacher in Evangelism

The pastor serves as a model in the evangelistic ministry of the local church. He preaches to reach the lost. Witnessing is part of the life of the pastor. The pastor's concern and burden includes the lost. These and other practices demonstrate for others in the congregation what it means to be committed to the fulfillment of the Great Commission.

The pastor also is an organizer in the evangelistic ministry of the church. In some situations, the pastor is the primary organizer. In other contexts, others may provide leadership in the evangelistic task. Nevertheless, the pastor must be involved in the organization and maintenance of the evangelistic ministries of the church. His role and leadership as pastor and shepherd is irreplaceable. Many times his influence and exhortation makes the decisive difference in the function of the evangelistic endeavor.

The pastor finally must participate in the teaching aspect of the evangelistic ministry of the local church. Soulwinning and discipleship are tasks that require instruction and training. The pastor as teacher in this process can be very effective. Not only does he fulfill his calling as pastor, but he also fulfills the evangelistic aspects of that calling. While he may be directly involved in evangelism, through instruction his efforts are multiplied as the sheep are equipped by the shepherd to bring others into the fold.

The Task of the Pastor as Evangelist As Found in the Book of Acts

In the Book of Acts, the use of the term *preach* provides a paradigm for the task of evangelism. In some translations the longer phrase "preach the good news" appears. At other times, just the word *preach* appears. In either case, *preach* is actually from *euaggelizo*, the Greek term from which *evangelize* comes. Therefore, *preach* is more specifically a reference to evangelization by means of the gospel.

The various contexts in which the terms and phrases mentioned above occur in Acts offer a rich paradigm for the task of evangelism. Each provides a different perspective of that task. When the Christians in the early church were dispersed because of persecution, they evangelized wherever they went. Their time of distress was turned into opportunities for evangelism (8:4). The church evangelized even in the face of the enemy (8:9-12). Evangelization was a continual task of the church (8:25, 40). Evangelism was done one-on-one by individuals as well as preached to the crowds (8:35). Evangelism was part of the proclamation of the lordship of Christ (10:36). Evangelism was presented across cultural lines (11:19-21). Evangelism was the message of the Resurrection (13:32, 33).

Evangelism was part of the ministry presented, even to those who came for healing (14:7-10). Evangelism was part of the outreach to cults and pagan religions (14:15). It was the message declared in the midst of victory over persecution (14:21). Part of the task of teaching included evangelism (15:35). Evangelism was at the heart of the missionary call (16:10). Finally, evangelism was not stopped, even though there were skeptics who tried to hinder it (17:18).

These passages indicate the effective fulfillment of the call to evangelize. The evangelization of the gospel was an important part of the early church. It was the means of the expansion of the church. It was part of the ministry of the saints, both in leadership and in service. Rather than being just a small addition to the ministry of the church, evangelism was at the heart of the church's power and mission.

A Theology of Revival

Revival has been interpreted in a number of different ways. Some feel that it is a spontaneous event that cannot be programmed or scheduled. Others feel that revival is a renewal of those who already believe, while evangelism is for the saving of the lost. From another perspective, some understand revival as a series of meetings for both the saving of the lost and the renewal of the saints—two distinct and separate events.

The essential definition adopted in this chapter will be

that revival is the renewing power of God in which believers are revived and the lost come to Christ. A number of biblical passages record revival events. Two will be examined: (1) the renewal experienced under the reign of Hezekiah (2 Chronicles 29; 30) and (2) the revival that came to the believers in Ephesus under Paul's ministry (Acts 19).

Renewal in the Kingdom of Hezekiah

Second Chronicles 29 and 30 records one of the greatest revivals in Judah. The entire nation was turned around spiritually under Hezekiah's reign. Perhaps the only other revival that reached a similar magnitude was the one that occurred under King Josiah.

The first theme of Hezekiah's revival was preparation for revival. He repaired and cleansed the house of the Lord (29:3-5). He gathered those in charge of maintenance of the Temple and assigned them tasks to do. Hezekiah challenged the leadership to cleanse themselves and draw close to God (vv. 6-11).

Preparation is a part of revival. This requires preparation by the leadership of the church. Many times, the worship team, the pastor, and other leaders begin the initial stages of revival through personal renewal. The house of God needs to be consecrated. A sense of the reverence of God and worship before Him should be reestablished if it has diminished. These were the initial steps of Hezekiah's revival.

The second theme that was prominent in Hezekiah's revival was cleansing from impurities. *Filthiness* (29:5) had come into the Temple and the lives of the people. In verse 7 Hezekiah declared some of the things that had led them to the need for revival. They had shut the door (lost the priority of spirituality); they had not kept the lamps burning (did not foster God's presence); they had not burned incense (did not honor the Lord); and they had failed to burn offerings (failed to confess sin). These represent areas in need of renewal and cleansing.

The third element of Hezekiah's revival was personal determination. Hezekiah made a personal covenant with the Lord (29:10). Regardless of what the others around him were going to do, Hezekiah pursued renewal. He was determined to be faithful in seeking revival. He encouraged those around him to be faithful. He did not ignore them but encouraged them. Nevertheless, his personal determination was sure.

The fourth element in Hezekiah's renewal was repentance before the Lord (29:20-24). This was initiated first by Hezekiah and the worship leadership of the Temple. The rest of the nation would eventually join them. Similarly, renewal and repentance by the pastor and those in leadership in the church paves the way for further repentance. Just as the people would eventually follow Hezekiah in repentance, the unbelieving world is waiting for a repentant church. The repentance of the church can become the catalyst for the repentance of the lost.

A fifth element in Hezekiah's revival was a return to obedience. God had commanded that certain things be done in worship and service to Him. These had been neglected. Their spiritual depravity was not the result of a lack of information. Neither was it because of a lack of opportunity. Essentially, it was due to a lack of obedience. Now that they had been repentant, they were willing to be obedient to the Lord once again (29:25-31).

The sixth element of Hezekiah's revival was the propagation of the Word of the Lord. They sent out letters (30:1), calling others to repentance and service unto the Lord. This is a necessary part of revival. If something is happening in the local church, the word of renewal needs to be spread. This is the gospel and evangelistic mandate today (Matthew 28:18-20). Especially during times of revival, when God is pouring out His Spirit, the church needs to spread the Word of the Lord and invite others to come (2 Chronicles 30:1-12).

The seventh element of the revival was spreading the impact of the revival beyond the walls of the sanctuary. The congregation took the spirit of revival into Jerusalem and the nation. They cleansed and purified the country of things that were not pleasing to the Lord (30:13-16). This was done by the people of God and not by any special group. In the midst of revival, people are stirred to a renewal of works for the Lord. They should be encouraged to spread the effects of the revival outside the four walls of the church.

These themes of Hezekiah's revival speak to the church today. Nothing can replace renewal within the hearts of the leaders of the church. It becomes a catalyst for revival. The themes of repentance, cleansing, and obedience are essential for salvation. As the church leads the way in the renewal of these attributes, the world will be drawn to believe in Christ. Revival can spread beyond the church walls as the church spreads the news and the impact of the revival into the world. Revival changed the nation of Judah under Hezekiah, and it can change a community and a nation today.

The Power of God in the Revival at Ephesus

Acts 19 chronicles a revival that took place under the ministry of Paul. This revival was especially marked by the manifestation of the power of God. People were baptized in the Holy Spirit (v. 6). The Word of God was boldly proclaimed (v. 8). Though there was opposition to the revival and the Word (v. 9), Paul continued to exhort and proclaim the Word. God used him mightily and "wrought special miracles by the hands of Paul" (v. 11). Many souls were brought to the Lord and the Word of God had a great impact on the area (vv. 18-20). The revival and renewal lasted for two years.

The principles recorded during this time in Paul's ministry in Ephesus apply to revival in the church today. Believers today, like the believers in Ephesus, need to experience the baptism in the Holy Spirit and the power of God in the midst of renewal (vv. 2-6). Many people need the power of God to be manifest in their lives for healing and many other needs (v. 12). People who are lost need the persistent proclamation of the message of salvation (v. 10).

The emphasis of this extended time of renewal was the power of God. Paul was the instrument God used. Through his ministry, the power of the Spirit baptized and filled believers. The power of God drew souls to understand the preached and taught Word. The power of God confronted the opposition and brought victory to the church. Through the power of God, the entire community of Ephesus and the surrounding region witnessed the impact of the Word of God. The power of God versus the power of men is a key insight of revival.

3

MINISTRY
TO
INDIVIDUALS
AND
FAMILIES

Pastoral Care and the Process of Grieving

9

The purpose of this chapter is to look at the relationship between the process of grieving and pastoral ministry. Much of pastoral care and counseling ministry is done for those who are in great need. Depression, despair, anxiety, crisis, and many other conditions beset people in need of the care of a pastor. The dynamics of these conditions can be understood many times by looking at the process of grieving. Grieving is an overall response to a number of different kinds of problems. Understanding the grief process can be beneficial for the pastor as he counsels individuals and families.

General Definition of Grief

Grief can be defined as the loss of anything or anyone meaningful in our lives—such as friends, spouse, children, home, job, material comforts, health, money, face, or security. People spend a good part of their lives seeking those things and relationships they feel will make life meaningful. When any of these are lost, it triggers a sense of grief.

A loss may not necessarily initiate an experience of grief. However, if much meaning is attached to the loss, a grief reaction is likely. This does not mean that a person is fated to despair. Rather, grief is part of the human experience.

Grief is not contrary to what Scripture reveals about human experience. Some have felt that grief is contrary to scriptures such as 1 Thessalonians 4:13: "Sorrow [grieve] not, even as others which have no hope." This verse is not an admonition not to grieve. Rather, it merely indicates that you are not to grieve as those who have no hope. The believer, in the midst of his grief, is to maintain his hope of eternal life.

The Scriptures are full of references to grieving and mourning. There are at least 29 different terms for *grief* in the Old Testament and many others in the New Testament. Both Testaments have many references for *mourn*.

Words for *Grieve* or *Grief* in the Old Testament

1. *'adab*—whine, high-pitched whine; 1 Samuel 2:33
2. *chuwl*—pain; Esther 4:4
3. *chalah*—weak, feeble; Amos 6:6; Nahum 3:19
4. *charah*—warm, anger; 1 Samuel 15:11
5. *raa*—tremble, fearful; Genesis 21:11, 12; Nehemiah 13:8
6. *kabad*—heavy; Genesis 12:10; 18:20; 41:31; Exodus 8:24
7. *ka'as*—turbulence, anger; Job 6:2, grief; Job 5:2, wrath
8. *la'ah*—weary, disgusted; Job 4:2; Proverbs 26:15
9. *marah*—rebel, bitter; Lamentations 1:20

10. *marats*—sharp, vehemence; 1 Kings 2:8

11. *chata'*—miss the mark, sin; Lamentations 1:8

12. *chamets*—to be sour, great vexation, especially internally; Psalm 73:21

13. *yagah*—to be afflicted with grief and anguish; Jeremiah 45:3; Lamentations 3:32, 33

14. *ka'ab*, great suffering and grief; Job 2:13; 16:6; Ezekiel 28:24

15. *ka'ah*—sad or fainthearted; Daniel 11:30

16. *kara*—to be pained, sorrowful; Daniel 7:15

17. *ma'al*—a trespass which is grievous; Ezekiel 14:13

18. *marar*—to be bitter; Genesis 26:35; 49:23; Ruth 1:13; 1 Samuel 30:6

19. *cuwr*—to turn aside, depart, revolt; Jeremiah 6:28

20. *'agam*—to be sad, sorrowful; Job 30:25

21. *'amal*—wearisome, labor, trouble, adversity, oppression, injustice; Isaiah 10:1; Habakkuk 1:3

22. *'atsab*—to labor, to be in suffering and pain, especially internally; Genesis 6:6; 34:7; 45:5; 1 Samuel 20:3; 20:34; 2 Samuel 19:2; Proverbs 15:1 (frequently used word)

23. *'athaq*—hard things; Psalm 31:18

24. *puwqah*—to cause someone to move back and forth, to stumble, to put an obstacle in someone's way; 1 Samuel 25:31

25. *quwt*—to grow tired of a thing, despise; Psalms 95: 10; 119:158; 139:21

26. *quwts*—to grow weary by a thing; Exodus 1:12

27. *qatsar*—to be shortened, to grow impatient and troubled; Judges 10:16

28. *qashah*—to be hard or cruel; 1 Kings 12:4; Isaiah 21:2

29. *ra'*—evil; Nehemiah 2:10; Jonah 4:6

Words for *Mourn* in the Old Testament

1. *ebel*—wail, weep; Genesis 27:41

2. *'anah*—groan intentionally; Isaiah 19:8

3. *bakah*—weep; Genesis 50:3

4. *caphad*—beat the chest, bereavement; 1 Kings 13:29

5. *ruwd*—wander; Psalm 55:2

Words for *Grief* in the New Testament

1. *lupeo*—sorrow; Mark 10:22; Hebrews 12:11; 1 Peter 2:19

2. *stenazo*—groan, sigh; Hebrews 13:17

3. *sullupeo*—to grieve with another person; Mark 3:5

4. *diaponeo*—to labor through; Acts 4:2; 16:18

5. *barus*—heavy, oppressive; Acts 20:29; 25:7; 1 John 5:3

Words for *Mourn* in the New Testament

1. *pentheo*—bewail, cry aloud; James 4:9; Revelation 18:8

2. *threneo*—grief, lament; Matthew 11:17; Luke 7:32

3. *kopto*—to beat the chest in grief; Matthew 24:30

4. *odurmos*—lamentation; Matthew 2:18; 2 Corinthians 7:7

Scripture gives no prohibition against the grieving process. The emphasis of Scripture is that the child of God must depend on God in the process of grief.

The process of grief as defined in this chapter is illustrated on the following page.

The Stages of Grief

Grief occurs in three stages: initial, middle, and latter stage. Each stage is distinctive, though a person may fluctuate back and forth between stages for a time. Grief may last only for a few days or it may last for a prolonged period of time. Some people may remain in the middle stages of grief for some time. This is the deepest and most despairing part of the process in the middle stage. To progess in the recovery process one must move toward the latter stage of grief.

The Initial Stage of Grief

The initial stage of grief begins with the loss itself. Loss can come from a variety of sources. The most descriptive element of this initiating event is that the person or thing lost had a significant meaning for the person.

After the onset of the loss, the initial stage is marked by a number of factors. They may not all occur. However, they are generally all possible. These symptoms include denial, shock, emotional release, physical symptoms, guilt, hostility, resentment, and anger.

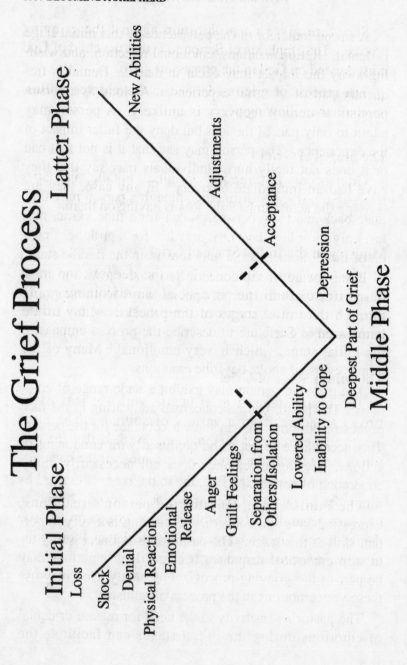

The Grief Process

Initial Phase

Loss
Shock
Denial
Physical Reaction
Emotional Release
Anger
Guilt Feelings
Separation from Others/Isolation
Lowered Ability
Inability to Cope
Deepest Part of Grief

Middle Phase

Depression
Acceptance
Adjustments
New Abilities

Latter Phase

A strong indicator of the persistence of this initial stage is denial. Rationalizations, emotional rejection, and wishing away the impact may occur in denial. Denial is frequently part of the grief experience. As long as a person persists in denial, recovery is unlikely. A person may admit to only part of the loss but deny the fuller impact of the experience. The person may say that it is not that bad or it does not really hurt. Individuals may say that they have had an immediate recovery. In any case, they are denying the actual impact the loss is having on them.

Ministry in the Initial Stage of Grief

Being aware of the concern Scripture shows for grief, the pastor can minister in special ways to those going through the initial stages of the process. Many of the terms used in Scripture to describe the process emphasize the initial stage, which is very emotional. Many of the terms reviewed above describe emotions.

The grieving person may exhibit a wide range of emotions. The pastor can be concerned and caring in the face of these emotions. He can show acceptance for the person. This acceptance is not to be confused with condoning of actions. Caring acceptance does not necessarily imply condoning of actions.

The minister can monitor the person's reactions, expressing love and concern. Monitoring is a very important skill at this stage. The pastor does not necessarily try to stop emotional responses because these emotions may be part of the grieving process. Frequently, God may use these very emotions in the process of ministry.

The pastor's sensitivity to the need for release or denial of emotions during the initial stages can facilitate the process. The pastor can minister through acts of love. Even though the person may be showing forms of denial, the pastor can assure the person of his availability.

When the tragedy of the loss does hit a person, the love of the pastor will be a strong incentive to contact him. The pastor can show love by attending to the physical needs of the person. The loss may be so great that a person neglects basic physical needs such as food, health, and proper rest. Being available in love during the initial stages opens the door for further involvement in the middle stages.

The Middle Stage of Grief

Entry into the middle stage of grief is marked by increased feelings of isolation and separation from others. An individual may intentionally separate himself, or circumstances may put him in isolation. Frequently, a person will feel isolated though surrounded by people. However a person may arrive at the condition and/or perception of separation from others, it indicates that he is moving toward the middle stage.

In the middle stage, a person will experience several other symptoms. A lowered level of efficiency is typical. This does not mean inactivity but a reduction in the level of activity. A person may lose touch with some aspects of what was previously normal or routine for him. He may not be able to relate to others or do the same kind of things he was able to do before.

The most critical part of the middle stage is when a person hits bottom. A person may go back and forth between the initial and middle stages for a time. However, when he reaches a state of deep and constant depression, he probably has entered more fully into the middle stage. This deepest part of the middle stage is marked by the inability to cope with other lesser problems as well. The individual feels an extreme loss of almost all hope. The fuller impact of the loss has finally hit.

Ministry in the Middle Stage

Ministry during the middle stage is very important. This is the time when the person has the greatest potential for beginning recovery. At the same time, it is the most discouraging time for the individual. The middle stage is the time when the greatest dependency upon the work of God is required. It is also the stage when a pastor may feel there is little he can do. The circumstances and emotions of the grief appear to be the most overwhelming at this stage.

The pastor should watch for the strength and nature of the person's relationships with others. The middle stage is begun with increased isolation and separation from others. The minister should be aware if the person shows decreased levels of dependency and interaction with others. If the person becomes more possessive, it may be an indication of greater self-centeredness. This may be a form of self-inflicted isolation. In general, the pastor can be on the alert for any movement a person makes away from others.

As the middle stage becomes more apparent, the pastor can monitor the individual's own self-perception. He may become completely focused upon his personal needs. This may be a form of isolation. The person may become apathetic about God. This also is an indicator of the middle stage. Anger toward God does not indicate isolation. However, apathy does. The person may speak of the loss in more personal terms. This may indicate loneliness and isolation. He may perceive the loss as being completely unique and different from anyone else's grief. This is another form of isolation.

The Latter Stage of Grief

The latter stage of grief is marked by acceptance and recovery. The person has stopped denying and started accepting the loss. The individual has experienced the deep valley of near loss of hope. A renewed sense of hope is coupled with the acceptance that things will not be the same. There is a change. With acceptance of this change brought about by the loss, the individual is able to develop new ways of coping and dealing with life. There is an adjustment to the loss. New abilities are formed to deal with stressors that lie ahead.

In the latter stage the person is not necessarily stronger, but there is an abiding strength there that was not there previously. It is a new strength. This strength is like new life because it has come out of the death and loss of the past. The new abilities the person has learned are not necessarily better, but they are new. They have profound meaning, because they are what has been retained as a result of the loss. They are valuable because the person needs these new abilities to continue life after the loss.

Ministry in the Latter Stage

Individuals move into the latter stage of the grief process when they have passed through the other two stages. There has been the time of emotional release in the initial stage. The denial of the initial stage has now turned into acceptance. There has been the bottom of grief and the heartfelt cry. The loneliness of the middle stage has turned into rejoicing and new relationships.

The grieving ones may have touched upon the latter stage to some extent earlier in the process. They were able to accept some of what was happening. There was a sense of some level of adjustment. However, they probably had not come fully through the other two stages. As a result, they moved back and forth. However, once the other two stages have been more fully experienced, they are now ready to more fully enter into the latter stage.

Ministry during the latter stage seeks to equip the person with new ways of coping. The tragedy of the loss took away some of the things that may have worked for the person in the past. Since the loss, relationships and habits have changed. It is a time of adjustment. Ministry during this stage equips the person for adjustments such as new relationships, a new job, or new surroundings.

The individual also needs to know how to look upon the past loss and grief. The grief of the past is not forgotten. However, it is transformed. What once was terrible tragedy has now become testimony and witness. The person remembers how he was sustained by God and those around him, though there is still pain in remembering. Nevertheless, there is a realization that the person is on the other side of the initial and middle stages. And there is a confidence that God has made recovery possible.

Three critical areas constitute much of ministry during this stage. First, the pastor can assist the person in developing a new network of supportive relationships, in which other people can give prayerful support. Second, the pastor can teach, train, show, and model ways to adjust. These include new skills, new habits, and new ways to work. Finally, the pastor can offer the new perspective of testimony and insight. Instead of constantly being despondent, the individual learns new ways to feel and respond.

The Ministry of God's Comforting Presence

> Blessed be God, even the Father of our Lord Jesus
> Christ, the Father of mercies, and the God of all com-
> fort; who comforteth us in all our tribulation, that we
> may be able to comfort them which are in any trouble,
> by the comfort wherewith we ourselves are comforted of
> God. For as the sufferings of Christ abound in us, so
> our consolation also aboundeth by Christ (2 Corinthians
> 1:3-5).

The ministry of comfort is important throughout the
grief process. In all stages, the pastor should endeavor to
show the kind of care mentioned in this passage. In the
initial stage it is important to exhibit care and support for
someone experiencing denial and trauma. In the middle
stage, care and comfort are needed for someone making a
heartfelt cry to God. In the latter stage the task is to con-
sistently show a person how to make new adjustments to
his loss. In each of these, a foundation of ministry is the
very presence of God. Second Corinthians 1:3-5 illustrates
how comfort can be applied in each stage.

The term *comfort* (*paraklesis*) in this passage in the
Greek comes from the same term as *exhort* (*parakaleo*)
found in 1 Peter 5:1, which is a compound construction of
two shorter Greek terms, *para* and *kaleo*. *Para* means
"alongside of." *Kaleo* means "to call." The combined
meaning is "to call someone to your side." The comfort
expressed is the kind of comfort that comes by virtue of the
presence of another.

Other terms that are not used in 2 Corinthians 1:3-5 for
comfort illustrate different kinds of comfort. Three other
terms used in the New Testament are translated "comfort."
The first is *paregoria*. This term, used in Colossians 4:11,

emphasizes comfort which "soothes or deadens pain."
Another term translated "comfort" is *paramutheomai*. It
means "comfort that encourages" and is used in John,
1 Corinthians, Philippians, and 1 Thessalonians. This kind
of comfort seeks to motivate and strengthen. A final term
translated "comfort" is *tharseo*. It is used in the Gospels
and Acts and indicates "comfort which endeavors to cheer
the emotions."

The use of *parakaleo* means that a very specific kind of
comfort is being communicated. This kind of comfort is
the deepest and most meaningful kind of comfort. The
other terms emphasize various areas of comfort. Freedom
from pain and release for the physical part of the person is
the specialty of *paregoria*. The inspiration of the heart and
the emotions is the focus of *paramutheomai* and *tharseo*.
Parakaleo includes these and more. The presence of a person brings comfort that ministers to the physical, emotional, and other aspects of a person's grief. It includes the
complete grief experience of the person.

Presence assures the person on emotional, physical, and
spiritual levels. The presence of another, especially the
Lord, assures a person that he is not alone. This kind of
comfort heals emotional hurts brought on by the loneliness
of a loss. Presence also brings physical confidence in
response to danger and peril from neglect. When a person
is in the deepest part of the middle stage, very little can be
explained emotionally or physically. A person has probably given all the thought he can to the loss. At that point,
the presence of the Lord and others can bring a comfort of
the Spirit that goes beyond intellect.

In 2 Corinthians 1:3-5 Paul declared that God has all the
comfort needed for any trouble. "The God of all comfort"
is an inclusive declaration meaning that whatever comfort

is required most, God's presence supplies. The phrase "in all our tribulation" is also inclusive. It means that the comfort of God meets the deepest need. These broad, all-inclusive claims are made by Paul because God's presence does indeed minister to any loss. His presence is the key to all the stages of grief.

The ministry of the pastor and other believers is applied in verse 4. Paul said the purpose of much of God's comfort toward us is that we may be able to comfort others. God equips the pastor to comfort others no matter what the grief. God uses the comforting process that occurs in the pastor's own life.

The pastor must be open to God's comfort in his own life and be willing to use that as a resource for counseling and caring for others. This is not the same as saying, "I have experienced the same thing." This kind of statement focuses upon the content of a loss. Everyone experiences different kinds of losses. The focus of 2 Corinthians 1 is upon the comfort and presence of the Lord. This is universal. The experience of the presence of God to comfort someone can be universally applied.

God's Strength in the Midst of Grief

And he said unto me, My grace is sufficient for thee: for my strength is made perfect in weakness. Most gladly therefore will I rather glory in my infirmities, that the power of Christ may rest upon me. Therefore I take pleasure in infirmities, in reproaches, in necessities, in persecutions, in distresses for Christ's sake: for when I am weak, then am I strong (2 Corinthians 12:9, 10).

Recovery and renewal of strength is hard to visualize in the midst of grief. Because of the depth of the loss, it is difficult to comprehend how one can ever return to any level of functioning. That perception becomes even more critical in light of the nature of the grief process. A person will eventually feel the impact of the loss, creating weakness, discouragement, and frustration. In the midst of this, it is very difficult to understand how recovery is possible. Not only is this kind of perception true of the person going through the grief process, it may also be true of those around him.

Recovery in the Lord is always possible, and it takes place in the weakest moments of the individual. This is the power of 2 Corinthians 12:9, 10. Paul did not deny his weakness. He had just detailed his inability to find relief from the "thorn" that had been troubling him (vv. 6-8). Paul acknowledged his weakness, but he also identified the strength that is present in weakness. The strength of the Lord does not come after the trouble; it comes in the midst of the trouble. The power of the Lord did not come after Paul gained his strength back. It was there when he was at his weakest point.

Seeing the power of the Lord available to strengthen someone in the midst of weakness is very important. If a pastor does not see this, he may be looking for strength without seeing a person's pain. The church may focus upon the elimination of grief and not the experience itself. Recovery is real, but the middle stages of weakness and travail are also real. Paul serves as a model for pastoral ministry. Rejoicing is possible in the midst of pain. This is not to ignore the pain, but to perceive the ways in which the Lord gives strength.

A Theology of Grief and Care (Psalm 107)

The Goodness and Everlasting Mercy of God

Psalm 107 is a model for analyzing the work of God in the midst of grief and crisis. This psalm provides insight into the process of grieving by discussing five themes which mirror the various stages of the grief process. The psalm illustrates the work of God by showing that throughout the various symptoms and experiences of loss, God is active in the lives of those suffering. Not only is the sense of loss real in the psalm, but the celebration of victory is also real.

The psalm begins with a declaration of God's response to man in the midst of tragedy. (v. 1). The expected response to God is affirmed throughout the various stages of grief (vv. 2, 8, 15, 21, 30-32, 42, 43). The declaration affirms three aspects of God's character and care. These provide a way to understand the work of God in times of crisis.

The first aspect is God's *goodness*. The term for good in the Hebrew is *towb*, which emphasizes uprightness and completeness. The goodness of God is the assurance that God is working in all things for the purposes of His completeness and uprightness. This is not a guarantee of the absence of conflict. Rather, it is the guarantee that God is working for the complete recovery and wholesome renewal of the individual.

The second aspect emphasized in verse 1 is God's mercy. This term used is the Hebrew word, *checed*, which is usually translated "lovingkindness." This is the translation of the term in verse 43. This love and mercy emphasizes faithful relationship, not emotions. It is love demonstrated by faithfulness. The declaration is that in the midst of the loss, God will not leave or forsake an individual. He will be faithful in His love and presence.

The final aspect emphasized is that God's action is everlasting ("endureth for ever"). This term is from the Hebrew word *olam*, which literally means "to hide." The idea of being hidden applies here to the aspect of time. Time is hidden and unknown to a person. Therefore, the declaration is that God is God in the hidden future. The emphasis of the term is that God is the God of all hidden places. This includes the hidden past and present and the hidden places of the heart and human experience.

Throughout ministry in the process of crisis and grief, these affirmations can be made. The psalmist intentionally repeated the call to see these affirmations about God. This is important for ministry in grief and crisis. Though it may be difficult to see these aspects of God's care in the midst of weakness and tragedy, this may be the most important emphasis of the psalm.

Various Stages of Grief Reflected

Psalm 107 has five major sections. Each section contains a theme (e.g., *enemies*) which identifies with a particular place in the overall grief process (*enemies* represents the initial stage) and the process of grief in miniature within its section (i.e., all three stages of grief—initial, middle, and latter—are in each section.).

The following diagram illustrates the theme of each section and where it fits on the overall diagram of the grief process. The various subsections are listed with their verse locations. Also on the diagram is the central declaration of God's goodness, mercy, and everlasting work.

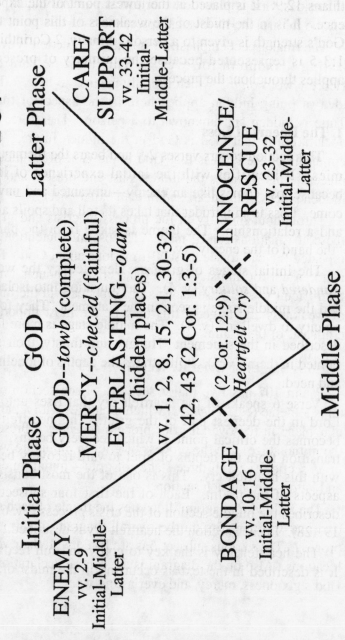

The Grief Process in Psalm 107

Initial Phase   GOD   Latter Phase

GOOD--*towb* (complete)
MERCY--*checed* (faithful)
EVERLASTING--*olam*
(hidden places)

vv. 1, 2, 8, 15, 21, 30-32,
42, 43 (2 Cor. 1:3-5)

ENEMY
vv. 2-9
Initial-Middle-
Latter

(2 Cor. 12:9)
Heartfelt Cry

BONDAGE
vv. 10-16
Initial-Middle-
Latter

INNOCENCE/
RESCUE
vv. 23-32
Initial-Middle-
Latter

CARE/
SUPPORT
vv. 33-42
Initial-
Middle-Latter

Middle Phase

Added to the diagram is a representation of 2 Corinthians 12:9. It is placed at the lowest point of the experience. It is in the midst of the weakness of this point that God's strength is given to a person. Finally, 2 Corinthians 1:3-5 is represented because the ministry of presence applies throughout the process.

1. The Enemy of Loss

This section covers verses 2-9 and bears the theme enemies. It identifies with the initial experience of loss, because loss comes like an enemy—unwanted and unwelcome. Loss is an intruder that takes its toll and spoils a life and a relationship. The theme is taken from the phrase "the hand of the enemy" (v. 2).

The initial stages of grief are depicted by the words *wandered* and *solitary* (v. 4). The transition into isolation and the middle stage is seen in the statement "They found no city to dwell in" (v. 4). The middle stage is more fully described in the statement "Hungry and thirsty, their soul fainted in them"(v. 5). It illustrates the depths of loneliness and need.

Verse 6 speaks of the heartfelt cry that rises unto the Lord in the deepest part of the grief. This heartfelt cry becomes the critical point at which recovery begins. The transition from the depths of grief toward recovery begins with this heartfelt cry. This is one of the most consistent aspects of the psalm. Each of the first four subsections describes the middle section of the crisis process (vv. 6, 13, 19, 28). In each section the heartfelt cry is described.

The heartfelt cry is the key to godly and full recovery. It is described in the text as occurring in the midst of, not after, the deepest part of the experience. The text reads, "Then they cried unto the Lord in their trouble." The heartfelt cry is not just a moment of emotional release or catharsis. It is a moment of faith. The grace and mercy of God is experienced. The person cries out, uninhibited by rationalizations or self-centered attempts at recovery. It is a moment of complete dependence upon God. For some it may be salvation. For others it may be a return to God. For still others it may be an experience of Christian growth. The cry cannot be reproduced through human methodology. It is a moment made possible only by the Spirit of God and the obedient response of the person in crisis.

After the heartfelt cry, the text describes the latter stage. The description is one of recovery and new adjustments. The following describe the dynamics of the latter stage: "He delivered them out of their distresses" (v. 6); "He led them forth by the right way. . . to a city of habitation" (v. 7); "He satisfieth the longing soul, and filleth the hungry soul with goodness" (v. 9).

The psalm calls the reader to remember the work of God in the midst of grief (v. 8). This call is repeated at the end of each subsection (vv. 8-9, 15-16, 21-22, 31-32, 42-43). Praise affirms the action of God in the midst of grief and crisis. It perceives the three attributes of God mentioned in verse 1. The recognition and praise of God is possible at any part of crisis. The praise does not deny the grief; rather, it recognizes God's work in the grief experience.

2. The Bondage of Isolation

The second section highlights the theme of isolation and bondage. This theme is indicative of the initial stage, especially as it moves toward loneliness and the middle stage. This subsection is found in verses 10-16. The idea of bondage is stated in verse 10—"bound in affliction and iron."

The various stages of the grief process are represented in the section. The initial stages of grief are represented in the phrases "sit in darkness," "in the shadow of death," and "bound in affliction and iron" (v. 10). The middle stage is represented with these words: "brought down their heart with labour," "fell down," and "there was none to help" (v. 12). The latter stage is found in verses 13, 14, and 16 in the following phrases: "out of their distresses," "out of darkness and the shadow of death," and "brake their bands in sunder." The heartfelt cry is in verse 13. The exhortation to praise the work of God in the midst of grief is in verse 15.

Critical issues that appear throughout all five subsections are rebellion and innocence. Sometimes grief is the result of rebellion and transgression. This is the case in the sections on bondage and hopelessness. At other times, grief comes upon those who are innocent. This is the case in the sections on enemies and the innocent. The final section, on the abiding care and support of God, emphasizes God's sovereign action in response to the finiteness of man.

3. The Hopelessness of Despair

The third section highlights the theme of hopelessness and despair. This theme is indicative of the depths of the middle stage. There is a fuller sense of frustration and tragedy at this point. This subsection is found in verses 17-22. The idea of hopelessness is stated in verse 18—"they draw near unto the gates of death."

The various stages of the grief process are represented in the section. The initial stages of grief are represented in these words: "afflicted" (v. 17) and "Their soul abhorreth all manner of meat" (v. 18). The middle stage is represented in these words: "They draw near unto the gates of death" (v. 18). The latter stage is found in verses 19 and 20: "He saveth them out of their distresses. He sent his word, and healed them, and delivered them from their destructions." The heartfelt cry is in verse 19. The exhortation to praise the work of God in the midst of grief is in verse 21.

4. The Rescue of the Innocent

The fourth section highlights the theme of rescuing the innocent. This theme is indicative of passage from the middle stage to the latter stage. This subsection is found in verses 23-32. The idea of the innocent is stated in verse 23. Those in distress find themselves in "great [and perilous] waters" because it was their "business" to be there. They did not ask to be there. It was a necessity. It was their vocation. They are innocent of rebellion or transgression. This could apply to marital relationships, parent-child relationships, vocation, and many other situations

The various stages of the grief process are represented in the section. The initial stage and the circumstances that bring the grief are described in verses 23-26a. These verses describe perilous waters and a storm that arises. The middle stage is represented in verses 26b and 27.

The description of the middle section is threefold. First, inner turmoil is described—"Their soul melted." Second, physical distress is described—"They reel to and fro, and stagger like a drunken man." Third, mental anguish is described—"at their wit's end."

The description of the latter stage is in verses 28-30. They describe God's bringing them safely to a desired place of haven. The heartfelt cry is in verse 28. The exhortation to praise the work of God in the midst of grief is in verses 31 and 32.

A critical issue concerns God's work in starting the storm (v. 25). There is no explanation. God is not defended. The section describes God's control and sovereign action over the storm. Sometimes the event which began a crisis or the grief process began with God. It may or may not be due to rebellion. Nevertheless, God is still sovereign. This is the major emphasis of the last section, God's loving sovereignty.

5. The Abiding Care and Support of God

The last section is a broad look at the work of God in grief and crisis. The work of God in the midst of blessing or tragedy is described. The initial, middle, and latter stages of the grief cycle are seen through rivers and waters turning to a wilderness and then prospering once again. Fields and livestock become barren and then are made bountiful again. Whether God is working to multiply greatly (v. 38) or to bring low (v. 39), He is still the same loving God declared throughout the psalm.

Seeing God's Work in the Midst of Grief

The concluding theme of the psalm is the necessity and reward of seeing God work in the midst of grief and crisis.

God has constantly been praised throughout the psalm for His works (vv. 8-9, 15-16, 21-22, 31-32, and 42-43). Verses 42 and 43 exhort the reader to constantly see God's loving care at work. The conditions of grief have been graphically described throughout the psalm. However, the reader is continually exhorted to keep seeing God's care in the midst of the tragedy as well as the triumph. When a person perceives this, there is a great blessing. The blessing is that "iniquity shall stop her mouth" (v. 42) and the "lovingkindness of the Lord" will be understood (v. 43). The reward is that the antagonism of grief will stop and the love of God will be experienced, no matter what the experience of grief may be.

Pastoral Care
for the Sick
and Dying

10

The rich man walked by Lazarus every day and did not pay attention to his condition (Luke 16:19-31). Lazarus was sick with ulcerations and sores (v. 20). This account had particular medical significance, and Luke is the only Gospel writer who records it. The rich man's neglect of Lazarus meant that the only relief Lazarus received came from the dogs that licked his wounds (v. 21). The tragedy of the rich man was not only his neglect of God but his neglect of Lazarus as well. This illustrates the importance of noticing, perceiving, and caring for the ill.

Sickness can be very frustrating and defeating. Illness is an intrusion, something the person did not ask for. The person has to do things about which he doesn't have a choice. These include changing his diet, adjusting behavior, taking medications on schedule, agreeing to medical procedures, being separated from loved ones, and a host of other things it is necessary for the sick to do.

The minister must endeavor to understand the sick person's world. The tendency is to be so caught up with our own priorities that, like the rich man, we bypass the needs of the sick. The rich man's self-centeredness kept him from caring for Lazarus. Self-centeredness is also at the root of most neglect of the sick. The pastor must especially work toward reaching out to the sick.

Ministering to Those Who Are Ill (Matthew 25:36)

Jesus placed a high priority on caring for the ill. In Matthew 25:21-46 there is a description of the end-time judgment. This description includes care for the sick. Jesus asked if time was taken to minister to the sick and said that ministering to the sick is an act of ministry unto Him.

The term *visit* (v. 36) is translated from the Greek word *episkeptomai*, which is composed of two Greek terms, *epi* (upon) and *skepas* (cover). The words in combination imply "to care for." Just as someone was protected and cared for by a covering, *visit* meant tending to a person's needs. Lazarus' sores needed attention, but the rich man did not notice or care for him.

Pastoral ministry to the sick is to lead the way in caring for the sick. Into the world of the ill, the pastor can bring the ministry of Christ. The pastor's care is an example to believers, causing the ill to receive not only comfort from the pastor but ministry from the church congregation as well.

The experience of illness has five common stages. At each stage, pastoral action is important. The first stage is the movement from health to sickness. Usually the pastor is unaware of this transition. However, if the pastor is aware of this shift, early ministry can be very helpful. The second stage is acceptance of the illness. The effective pastor will see the benefit of ministering during this stage. The person is dealing with the difficult reality of the condition. The third stage is when the illness has become severe and special medical care is needed. The pastor typically is involved by this point, but sometimes he must catch up on issues the sick person has been dealing with for some time.

The fourth stage is the time of recovery. This can be a lonely time because many people will think the person is already fully recovered. Actually, full health has not been achieved. The person is still subject to weakness, physically and emotionally, from the experience of the illness. This can be a most effective time of ministry. The support of medical specialists and friends may have faded by now. However, the pastor can still be available to offer empathy and care.

The final stage is health and recovery. If effective pastoral intervention has been given during the illness, the person will be able to integrate the illness as a testimony. The memory of pastoral care in the midst of need will be a significant milestone in their experience.

Understanding the Role and Motivation of the Minister

The minister must be careful to avoid selfish motivations. A sick person can easily detect if a minister feels forced to make a visit. If the pastor is not as concerned about the person as with other things, it can be easily detected. If there is an attitude of patronization, the person who is ill will feel diminished and put down. The pastor must avoid appearing to be in a hurry. Time must be taken to focus on the world of the person and the special care he needs.

Understanding the Role of Those in the Helping Professions

The minister can increase pastoral effectiveness by developing positive working relationships with health-care professionals. Be cautious about judging a hospital or clinic solely on the basis of what the patient may say. Be cordial and responsive to health-care personnel. Respect the posted rules of an institution. Exercise cordiality when communicating with medical staff. Be careful to identify the authority structure and chain of command in an institution. This means you know whom to ask certain questions. If you meet with resistance from personnel, usually it is an exception. Medical personnel can be very helpful and positive relationships build foundations for future ministry.

Guidelines for Ministering in the Hospital

The hospital can be an effective place for ministering. Certain guidelines are helpful in ministering in the hospital setting. The suggestions below give attention to the needs of the patient as well as the institution:

1. Find out where a patient is and the best time to call.

2. Dress appropriately, no extremes.

3. Gain information ahead of time about the person's illness and condition.

4. Note the feeling and atmosphere communicated by the room (cards, flowers, personal items, etc.).

5. Recognize where to sit and stand. It's usually best not to sit on the bed.

6. Excuse yourself if the doctor appears. Respect his need to see the person.

7. Excuse yourself if a meal is being served. It may be

more comfortable for the patient.

8. Excuse yourself if others come to visit and there may be too many visitors for the comfort of the person.

9. Do not follow the person's request for water, food, etc. Check with the nurse.

10. Do not give medical opinions or advice. That is not your area of expertise.

11. Do not talk with someone else about the person who is ill while you are in his presence. This applies even if the patient is in a coma.

12. Do not talk too much. Focus your attention on the patient.

Fears and the Experience of Dying

The person who is dying is usually facing a number of fears. These fears revolve around personal and relational issues. They may have very deep concerns that they have shared with no one. These fears are harbored and become a source of inner conflict. Pastoral ministry can emphasize availability and love for a person dealing with these fears.

One fear a dying person may face concerns things which may happen after death. The person may be wondering about the fate of his body. He may wonder where his body will be and what people will think about the condition of his body. Another issue is judgment after death. He may wonder if he is in right relationship with the Lord. A significant feature is the general fear of the unknown. The future feels very threatening because the person has no control over himself or events after death.

Other fears the person may face involve the process of dying. These may include the fear of pain. This can become a cycle in which fear of pain produces pain which in turn produces more anxiety about pain and the cycle is perpetuated. Another aspect of the process of dying concerns issues of dignity. The person may wonder how awful he looks and how other people see him in this condition? The dying person needs to be dressed, fed, even taken to the bathroom. He feels the loss of his personal dignity. Also, the dying become concerned that in the process of dying they become an increasing burden upon others.

A final series of fears revolve around the actual loss of life. The dying eventually lose more and more mastery and control over their life. They begin to feel extremely helpless and useless. They deal with feelings of incompleteness and failure. They wish they could have done more. They feel they should have done more. They have much anxiety about the inevitable separation from loved ones. Dying becomes a profound experience of loneliness.

Ministry in the midst of these fears must be very sensitive to the condition of the fears. The pastor may know a lot about the subject of dying. However, knowledge about what a particular person is experiencing can only come from that person. This means the pastor must do a lot of listening, trying to perceive and understand the individual experience of the dying person. If the pastor does not endeavor to understand the unique grief experience of the dying, he will only increase the loneliness of the individual. The specific understanding the pastor gives becomes a platform from which continued love and care can be given. Further, the model proposed in an earlier chapter about grief ministry can be applied from this platform of understanding.

Pastoral Care for the Bereaved

Ministry to the Bereaved

One of the most important events in ministering to the bereaved is the initial confrontation with the death. The moment of first receiving news of the death is critical. That moment is captured in the memory of the person. It has a profound impact upon the person then and in the future. It is at times a moment of strong trauma. Emotions become overwhelming. The person will be in some degree of shock. Ministry at this moment becomes very important. Ministry can become part of what the person remembers about the experience.

Part of the initial confrontation with the death includes the first viewing of the deceased. This may occur for the bereaved immediately after the death. The bereaved may even have been present with the person at death. Or the first viewing may be delayed until the body is in the funeral home. In any of these cases, the impact of seeing the person after death is a significant step. The trauma experienced is the physical identification with death. The person's death becomes a reality.

A variety of reactions are experienced during these first events. One person may become extremely emotional. Another individual may be very stoic and distant. Some people experience temporary shock, experiencing a kind of suspension from reality. Others may rationalize or exhibit some other form of denial. A common reaction is to immediately blame someone or something for the death. The most common denominator of these experiences is intensity. The experience, whatever it may be, will probably be a very intense one.

Ministry must focus upon the immediate needs of the

bereaved. The person usually needs much immediate empathy and care. It is not a time to try to work through their grief with a lot of answers. The focus is upon surviving the immediate trauma. The person is not focused upon the content of words. The emotional empathy of the pastor will be remembered the most.

Pastoral Care and Counseling of the Bereaved

Pastoral ministry for the bereaved must allow them to experience the loss. Though the bereaved person cannot avoid the reality of death, one of the greatest temptations is to deny the impact of the death. It usually is affecting them more than they realize. The pastor must see the weight of the death. Certainly, a person does not overcome the trauma of death within a few hours. Nor, is it an event that will be overcome within a few days.

Pastors can use the assurance of the salvation of an individual to reduce the impact of death on the loved ones. However, even though the person was saved and assured of a heavenly home, the individual will still be missed. Focusing upon eternal issues must not result in the neglect of temporal issues. Those left behind still have loneliness, despair, and many needs to confront in the absence of the loved one.

No one knows exactly when death will come. Therefore, death is often quite unexpected. The bereaved are to some measure unprepared, no matter what preparations have been made. Even if the person has made excellent financial arrangements in the event of death, other considerations such as emotional preparation, living arrangements, collecting insurance, and many other needs remain. Nor does the fact that preparations have been made mean that the bereaved are ready to handle them.

No amount of words, prayer, or Scripture reading will change the reality of the death or its circumstances. The function of ministry and the Word for the bereaved is to equip them in the midst of these realities. The basic conditions of death and bereavement cannot be changed. The dead will not return in this life, and the bereaved will walk alone. The minister can journey with the grieving ones, but he cannot take them off the road of bereavement.

The pastor should avoid stereotyping the experience of bereavement. Each individual, even within the same family, will grieve differently. The particular grief each person is experiencing must be considered. Such personal attention in and of itself communicates volumes of care and compassion. The pastor may not know what to do or how to respond in the case of each person. However, just the individualized perception and attention is an act of ministry and care.

At times, the dead will be idolized or made larger than life. The bereaved may also feel they could have done more for the deceased person and feel guilty about what was not done. The bereaved may try to relive events or mistakes they experienced with the person who is deceased. In these attempts, the bereaved may become controlled by the other person, even though he is deceased, and memory becomes selective and distorted.

Much of the idolization of the deceased is natural. It is traumatic to think that you will never be able to do what you always wanted to do or felt you should have done before the person died. These attempts to idolize the person come out of extreme pressure brought on by guilt or anger.

Idolization of the dead is a form of denial. The

bereaved may not want to admit certain events are not repeatable. They may feel driven to satisfy guilt or anger toward the deceased. The bereaved is not willing to face the reality and finality of the death.

Ministry to those trying to idolize or "bring to life" the deceased involves both the recognition of pain and the assurance that this is not necessarily a permanent condition. The pastor must exercise the compassion of Christ in perceiving the guilt and hurt from which such attempts come.

The temptation is to jump to a preliminary conclusion about the permanence of the condition. Just because the person is exhibiting this kind of denial does not mean that he will always do so. The task is to perceive any indications that the person is letting go of the denial. At those critical times, words of compassion can assure the person that the pastor, like the Good Shepherd, will be with the sorrowing one "through the valley of the shadow of death."

Ministry at the Funeral Service

The funeral service is an important part of the pastor's ministry to the bereaved. The focus of the service is not just a recognition of the life of the deceased. It is the interpretation of that person's life in light of the grief of those who are left behind. The bereaved will be greatly affected by the service. The funeral service is the formal recognition of their grieving process. Therefore, it is important that the minister offer words of comfort and assurance to those grieving, while eulogizing the person who has died.

The funeral can be a time of pastoral care and counsel. Personalizing the service can communicate a great deal of care. Rather than speaking of ideas or theological concepts, focus should be on this particular death and the specific experience, including the spiritual condition, of those left behind. Creating a sense of participation with those grieving can have the effect of care and love. Rather than keeping the bereaved at arm's length, perpetuating the denial they may be experiencing, invite them to help plan the content of the service. During the funeral, talk and participate with the bereaved rhetorically so as to invite them to join you in considering the death of the person.

Using prayer effectively during initial viewing of the deceased, visitation at the funeral home, and at the funeral can be some of the best opportunities for ministry. This would include prayer at the initial viewing of the body. Prayer at these times is in part an affirmation of the reality of death. Reference to this reality in the prayer helps persons confront their denial. Prayer also provides a divine and eternal context for what has happened. It causes individuals to realize that the finality of death on earth does not indicate that life is limited to the here and now. There is an eternity beyond death. Prayer is helpful in assuring the bereaved of the presence of God in the midst of their suffering.

The funeral can be an effective time for the body of Christ to minister to the bereaved. The acts of love and support during this time will have lasting value. The church can communicate its genuine love and concern for the bereaved through food gifts and flowers. However, the primary gift of the church to the bereaved is its presence. Other gifts should not be intended as substitutes for being present at the funeral home or at the funeral. These times are valuable opportunities when the sheer presence of individuals in the church will minister to the bereaved.

The pastoral sermon at the funeral must affirm both the reality of death and the reality of life beyond death.

Scripture does both. This is especially depicted in the death and resurrection of the Savior. His death is graphically described in the Gospels. The care taken in preparing His body, the burial scene, and the events surrounding His burial are all given in detail. No attempt is made to gloss over the reality of His death. However, the glory and truth of life after death is very much a part of the story. The reality of the Resurrection is given direct attention.

The reality of death can be communicated through the sermon in a number of ways. Specific accounts from the life of the individual can emphasize the reality of this person's death. References to the specific circumstances surrounding the person's death can further affirm its reality. The use of names and places makes what has happened in death a greater reality. These are the kinds of things that the Gospel writers did in recording Christ's death.

The reality of life after death can also be communicated in the sermon. Any testimony of the person's Christian faith can be shared. This assures the individuals present of the eternal destiny of the person. If the spiritual condition of the person was doubtful, references can still be made to the reality of life after death. No one should presume to know completely whether a person died with no hope of salvation. Such a profound judgment should be reserved only for God. Nevertheless, the issue of eternity and life beyond death must be addressed. This is part of the reality faced in recording Jesus' death and resurrection.

The pastor should be aware of the necessity for follow-up and continued care for the bereaved. Ministry to the bereaved prior to the funeral lasts only a few days. However, once the funeral is over, ministry does not stop. The dynamics of grief are very real. Continued ministry to the bereaved is just as important as the viewing and funeral.

Primary Principles
of
Pastoral Counseling

11

The purpose of this chapter is to define counseling that places first priority upon the person and presence of God. This is the essence of the shepherding task. In Ezekiel 34 and John 10, the summary declaration was that the people may know God. This is the goal of the shepherd of the people of God. The counseling proposed in this book advocates a God-centered approach to counseling.

Theocentric Counseling:
Counseling Centered in God

The term *theocentric* means "centered in God." Thus, theocentric counseling is defined as "counseling that is centered in God." Theocentric counseling endeavors to place God in the center of the counselor's life and counsel. It also seeks to place God at the center of the life of the counselee. The relationship between the counselor and the counselee is centered in God, meaning that the focus and direction of counseling come from God. Throughout the process of counseling, the presence and power of God is affirmed.

The pastor's responsibility to counsel is important. Individuals struggle with many needs. Many times the first and only person they seek out for counsel is the pastor. When counseling opportunities arise, the pastor must be ready to respond immediately, for the opportunity may not always be there. The person may not be as willing to seek counseling later, or circumstances may change.

The pastor's response needs to be focused upon God. Many institutions and helping professionals in the community are dedicated to assisting people with their needs and problems. Each one in the helping process is committed to certain goals and assumptions. However, no one else in the community is so dedicated to the will and action of God in this world as the pastor. The express purpose of the pastoral office is to shepherd individuals to a knowledge of God's presence and power.

Essentially four centers, or focal points, may be assumed in pastoral counseling. The first is the counselee. The counselor can assume that the needs and abilities of the client are more important than anything or anyone else in the counseling process. The second possible focal point is the counselor. In counselor-centered counseling, the counselor and the counselee assume that the key to recovery lies in the expertise of the counselor and the influence of the counselor on the counselee. The third possible focal point is the relationship between the pastor and counselee, assuming that the two are willing to work together.

The fourth focal point is the assumption that God is present, that He is at the center of the counseling process, and that He is directing it. The most important aspect of the counseling process is not the action or needs of the counselee, the ability of the counselor, or the relationship between pastor and counselee. Rather, recovery is assessed by, made possible by, and guided by the action of God. God does not necessarily condone all the actions, emotions, or advice of the counselor and counselee. However, God is active in the midst of the process. The counselor and counselee are not insignificant. On the contrary, their responsiveness is essential. Nevertheless, the center and source of care is God.

In the case of client-centered counseling, the first question asked in the counseling relationship is "What are the needs, abilities, and potentials of the client?" In counseling centered on the counselor, the first question asked is "What can I do to help this person?" In relational-centered counseling the first question is "What can we do together?" In theocentric counseling, which is centered on God, the first question to ask in counseling is "What is God doing in the midst of this person's life?"

Theocentric Method

This section will present the essential elements of a God-centered method of counseling. The various parts of the method will be described in more detail following this outline.

A God-Centered Model of Counseling

1. The counselor perceives the presence, power, and action of God as central and originating.
2. Identification of various areas:
   - Spirit and primary assumptions

- Emotions
- Thinking
- Behavior
- Context of things, people, and circumstances

3. Identification of levels of intervention:
   - Prevention and education
   - Meeting needs and correcting problems
   - Crisis intervention
4. Affirm all areas listed in number 2.
5. Monitor changes in levels in number 3.
6. Use of the language of the Word of God
7. Confession and testimony at summary moments
8. Devotion in the midst of counseling
9. Affirm the "mystery" and power of God's action.

The various items of the theocentric method do not have to be done in order, with the exception of the first item listed. The perception of the counselor is very important. The questions that are first asked and the initial assumptions that are made will guide the entire process. These first assumptions and perceptions need to be centered on God.

This first step does not always require verbalizing faith or God-centered perspective. But even without verbalization, the perspective of the counselor looks to God.

The other items listed can vary in order and priority. It is important to note that items 1 through 5 must all be done. If they are not all done, then God's work in the midst of the counseling process will be missed. Not all of items 6 through 9 need to be done, but at least some of them must be done. If they are all excluded, then it will be difficult to center upon God in the counseling process. The sooner any of these items are done, the more apparent the theocentric process will become.

A counselor does not have to do items 6 through 9 immediately. It may be possible to use them only over the course of time because of the spiritual condition of the person being counseled or the context in which the counseling is being done. However, some or all of these items have to eventually be done.

The Perception of the Counselor (Step 1)

The first step is important because the perspective of the counselor is important. It is very difficult for the counselee to see God at work in the midst of his problems unless he has the empathy and leadership of the counselor. Because the counselor influences the person being counseled, the perceptions and assumptions of the counselor will have perhaps the greatest impact on the person being counseled.

The pastor can develop this perception by constantly reminding himself of the need for this perspective. It must be a part of every session of counseling. It must be a part of the preparation of the pastor. And the pastor must exercise this discipline as part of his daily walk with the Lord for his own life.

Area of Spirit and Primary Assumptions (Steps 2 and 4)

The area with the most primary influence upon a person is the area of spirit and primary assumptions. These are listed under numbers 2 and 4 above. This is the most basic way in which a person sees the world. It is the level of character and intuitive insight. Most importantly, this is the level of the spirit where an individual communes with the Lord.

For the believer, this area is developed through a variety of means. These include prayer, silence, intercession, invitations to the work of the Spirit of God, manifestations of spiritual gifts, words of exhortation, and laying on of hands. These can be done individually or in the midst of counseling. They all serve to develop this area of a person's life.

The primary goal of this area is to see and experience God's work as central and originating. The counseling goal of each area is given in the chart on the next page.

Seeing God's work as central means that throughout the process of counseling and the various changes that may occur, the measuring line and guiding factor is God. Seeing God's work as originating means that God is at the beginning and ending of the process, giving power and sustenance in the process.

For the unbeliever, the lack of salvation does not mean that nothing can be done or that nothing will be accomplished. On the contrary, God is still moving in the midst of that person's life and the counseling process. Even if the person does not become saved during counseling, God still is working in the midst of the individual's need. This does not necessarily mean that God or the counselor is condoning the person's actions.

The task of the counselor is to address needs from the perspective of God's care and compassion. The unbeliever will feel the impact of that ministry and will experience some change. This is based upon the power of God's

Theocentric Areas and Goals	
Assumptive/Spirit	
Seeing God's Work as Central and Originating	
Emotion	
Recognize That God Created Emotions and Ministers to Them	
Thinking	
Subject One's Mind to the Will of the Lord in Obedience	
Behavior	
Learn as a Disciple From the Lord	
Context of People, Things, and/or Circumstances	
Recognize That God Is Active in the People and Context of the Counselee	

work. However, since the person does not know Christ as Savior, the most complete degree of change and fullest potential for recovery will not be achieved.

Area of Emotions (Steps 2 and 4)

Emotions are a very important part of the counseling process. People feel very strongly about issues they are dealing with, such as deep hurts from the past and the resulting bitterness. It may be difficult for the individual to share some emotions or to deal with them. The pastor should endeavor to effectively address these emotions as a part of counseling.

The goal of counseling in the area of emotions is to recognize that God both created emotions and ministers to them. The pastor can provide care which addresses the emotional condition of a person. This does not mean that the pastor condones every action of a person. But recognition of pain and the extension of compassion is necessary. God created people as feeling human beings, and compassion for individuals is a recognition of God's creation.

Area of Thinking (Steps 2 and 4)

The ability to think is a very important resource for the person being counseled. Events and issues need to be prioritized. They need to be set in order. The person needs to understand the issues related to his problems. Logic needs to be applied to the order and arrangement of things that have occurred. Insight and thought can be applied to past, present, and future events. Problems can be approached with reason and rationality.

Thinking can be an important resource for moving from

feelings to actions. The feelings a person has can be interpreted and understood by the mind. Determination can be
formulated. Intentions can be assessed. Analysis can be
applied. Appropriate behaviors can be selected.
Eventually, after processing emotions through the mind,
the best and most godly behaviors can be acted out.

The goal of this area is to subject one's mind to the will
of the Lord in obedience. The thinking ability of man is
emphasized in Scripture through concepts such as *mind*
and *will*. Scripture emphasizes the use of the mind (Isaiah
10:7; 1 Corinthians 14:14-19). The use of the will is also
emphasized (Malachi 1:10; Luke 23:25; John 8:44;
Romans 7:21; 2 Corinthians 8:11; Ephesians 2:3). The
emphasis of these themes is that the believer submit his
mind to the will of the Lord (Romans 12:1, 2; Philippians
2:1-8).

Area of Behavior (Steps 2 and 4)

If a person's behavior is not changed, very little real
change can be assured. Good feelings and thoughts remain
incomplete without matching behavior. The actions of an
individual reveal the condition of the heart (Matthew 12:34).
Intentions need to be carried one step further into actions.

The goal of this area is to learn from the Lord. The concept of *disciple* emphasizes Christ's teaching to those who
believed on Him. His teaching was not centered in intellectual content. Christ taught so that fruitful behavior
would result in a person's life (John 4:34-38; 15:14-16).

Area of Context (Steps 2 and 4)

This area involves the people and things that surround

the person being counseled. People are affected by their surroundings. No one develops problems in isolation, nor can they find an answer in isolation. The context of the individual always has an impact upon him.

The goal of this area is to recognize that God is active in the people and context around the person receiving counsel. He is speaking to hearts and moving upon the situations and circumstances surrounding them. This is an affirmation of the incarnate presence of Christ when He walked on earth. He demonstrated His power over the wind and the waves. This represented His control over the things that affect our lives. It is also an affirmation of the work of the Holy Spirit to move upon lives today. Finally, it is an affirmation of the sovereign action and control of God over this world.

Levels of Intervention and Counseling (Steps 3 and 5)

In this area of the counseling process, the pastor is aware of the severity of the person's need. If there is no immediate, pressing need, the person may need counseling on the level of education and information. This is an effort to prevent something more critical from happening. If there is an immediate need brought on by the occurrence of one or more problems, the person needs counsel on a more in-depth level. This requires attention to certain needs and the correction of problems. Finally, if there is an actual crisis where the individual is seriously threatened by a problem, immediate intervention is needed. Counseling should take the form of decisive action to help to meet problems that are a serious threat to the person.

The Language of the Word of God in Counseling (Step 6)

The pastor must be cautious about using terms and definitions in counseling. Certain terms which diagnose a person's condition, such as *functionality, family system*, or *depression*, do not necessarily represent anything opposed to a God-centered approach to counseling. However, any term or the use thereof which does not seek after the action and centrality of God can threaten the counseling process.

One assurance of focusing the counseling process upon God is to use the terminology of Scripture at decisive moments. A family may be *dysfunctional*, but the root problem may be one of *transgression*. The former is a term used in certain types of marital counseling, while the latter is a description from Scripture. One of the most important reasons for using scriptural terms is that they remind a person of the priority God has for his life. They place the focus on God and not human ability or insight.

The role of the Word of God in the areas of spirit, emotions, thinking, behavior, and context can be illustrated in 2 Timothy 3:16, 17. The Word of God is presented as the basis for change in individual lives. In that passage, *inspiration* and *doctrine* relate to spiritual direction and priorities. *Reproof* refers to confrontation which affects the emotions and sentiments of the heart. *Correction* calls for logical changes which will change and reshape the will of an individual. *Instruction* addresses the need to learn new behaviors that are consistent with the Word. Finally, *furnished* refers to the practical and effective use of these changes in the circumstances of life.

Confession and Testimony at Summary Moments (Step 7)

When there is a sense of new awareness or accomplishment in the counseling process, it is important to use it as an opportunity to refer to the work of God. Confession is the admission of one's dependence upon God. This may be when a person comes to the Lord in repentance. Or it may be a time to confess faith and one's need of God. Testimony is a declaration that God is the principal reason for what has been accomplished. The pastor and the person receiving counsel were involved. However, God was the One who made the actual change possible.

Devotion in the Midst of Counseling (Step 8)

Devotional moments in the midst of counseling provide opportunities for spiritual awareness and spiritual priorities to be developed. Moments of prayer emphasize that God is present now and in the future, working in the life of the counselee. Times of praise and worship recognize the power of God and the honor due Him in the midst of the process. Without such devotional moments the counseling time could focus only upon the accomplishments of the pastor or the counselee.

Affirm the Mystery and Power of God's Action (Step 9)

God's action cannot be fully discerned or understood. Whenever God works in the midst of a life, there will be a feeling of mystery. *Mystery* means that something is hidden and not fully revealed. Part of the work of God is known through the Scripture, the Spirit, and God's work in creation. However, all is not known about God or the ways in which He works. Examples in pastoral counseling would be the moment at which a runaway decides to come back home or a wayward spouse decides to be faithful. These moments when the most significant changes occur cannot be totally explained by areas such as intellect or emotions. They remain part of the mysterious yet wonderful action of God.

A genuine dependence upon the work of God will be demonstrated by faithful obedience to all areas—spirit, emotions, thinking, behavior, and context. If an individual claims to be faithful in trusting God to act in a situation but does not obey in all the areas mentioned earlier, the level of faith must be put in question. This is the principle of faith and works James spoke about (2:14-18). This means that the pastor in counseling must work at helping a person to develop in all the areas of life: spirituality, emotions, thinking, behavior, and context of relationships and circumstances. For example, individuals may claim spiritual maturity, but if their love and relationships with others has not increased, their maturity is in question (John 13:34, 35).

The theocentric method is intended to remind the pastor and counselee that God is active in the midst of the counseling process. The various areas listed under step 2 may be developed individually with the assistance of special methods that emphasize a particular area. For example, certain techniques from family counseling methods may enhance the area of context. The theocentric method emphasizes that guidance and the direction of the use of other methods comes from God. God is maintained as the One who is at the center of the process and the One who gives direction throughout the process.

Pastoral Care for Families and Couples

12

This chapter introduces important biblical themes that concern the family. They can serve as a theological foundation for approaching family issues in counseling. They can also serve as the basis for enrichment and educating the local church about the family. The themes particularly integrate the Christian life and faith with family living.

Relationship Between Personal and Family Commitments (Joshua 24)

Commitment is often interpreted as an individualistic issue. The assumption is made that people exist as individuals with no attachments. Decisions and choices are assumed possible without any regard for heritage, home, or responsibilities to others. In particular, individual choices are treated as void of family contingencies.

To the contrary, the commitment asked for in Joshua 24:15 is both a personal and family commitment. The two cannot be separated. Individuals do not live completely to themselves. Individual choices always affect others, especially family members. Conversely, family commitments affect individual members. Joshua expressed his commitment as both a personal and family choice when he said, "As for me and my house, we will serve the Lord."

Spirituality Demonstrated in the Family (Ephesians 5:18—6:4)

In this passage spirituality is illustrated in two ways. Verses 19 and 20 describe spirituality demonstrated in worship. The terms *speaking* and *giving thanks* are circumstantial modifiers used to amplify the basic exhortation in verse 18 to be filled with the Spirit. The largest section of Paul's discourse, 5:21—6:4, describes the application of spirituality through submissive relationships in the family.

The term *submitting* (v. 21) is also a modifier of the basic exhortation to be filled with the Spirit. Submission applies to both persons in a relationship—"submitting yourselves one to another." The home is used to illustrate how individuals submit to one another in love, reverence, and obedience (5:33; 6:1).

The size and order of Paul's illustration of the family in this text directly implies that spirituality is especially exhibited through godly relationships in the family. His subject was spirituality. He briefly mentioned worship but spent the majority of time using submission within the family to illustrate the Spirit-filled life. If a person is truly spiritual, it will be lived out in family relationships. If a person does not exhibit proper family relationships, it is a statement about that person's spiritual condition.

Commitment to God's Work in the Family (The Book of Ruth)

The Book of Ruth is a family book, not just the story of one woman's commitment. The story begins with the description of a family and the tragedy it experienced (1:1-5). The story focuses upon the daughter-in-law and mother-in-law relationship of Ruth and Naomi. It later focuses upon another member of the extended family, Boaz. The answer to the calamity of the family is not Boaz's wealth but the birth of a child (4:13-22). The blessing that came to the family was that the family name would not be cut off (4:10).

The temptation is to look at Ruth as an individual and interpret the events as mere reflections of Ruth. However, the book is about the struggles and near-death of a family. The prophetic dimension of the book is that out of the faithfulness of the family—Ruth, Boaz, and Naomi, not just Ruth—the lineage of David and ultimately the Messiah continued. Family faith, not individualistic faith, is the story of the book.

Remaining Faithful When a Family Member Is Not Saved (1 Corinthians 7:10-24)

In this passage, Paul exhorted couples to faithfulness to one another. Despite the unfaithfulness of one spouse, his call is that the other spouse remain faithful. Verse 16 especially challenges the believer not to draw presumptuous conclusions about the future condition of the unbelieving spouse.

The theme of faithfulness can be applied to family members in general. The unbelieving family member may be a son, daughter, parent, sibling, or grandparent. The exhortation is to remain faithful to the family member and the family in general.

The exhortations are placed in the context of stewardship in verses 17-24. This was Paul's climactic appeal, taking up much of the section. Faithfulness is an act of stewardship based upon the believer's relationship with God (vv. 17, 22), not the acts or callings of men. The rewards of stewardship are grounded in the Lord. They are not dependent upon the relationship with the unbelieving family member.

Parent-Child Bonding

The parent-child bond is rooted in God's creative action in forming the family. Human procreation is not dependent upon the acts of men and women. Men and women are involved in human reproduction, but the moment of conception is still a miracle wrought by God. It is not subject to chance activity of cells, nor is it dependent solely upon the choices individuals make.

Children come as an inheritance from the Lord (Psalm 127:3). An inheritance is not dependent upon the recipient's action or merit. It comes through the benevolence of the donor. The one who gives children is God. He is the giver of the inheritance.

Parent-child bonding is related to the perception of God's gift of children. If children perceive themselves only as the product of human action, the triangle of God, parent, and child is significantly altered. No longer does primary dependence turn toward God. Rather, the child is turned to depend first upon the parent. Both the child and the parent feel that their destiny is in their own hands and not in the hands of God. God is not seen as the origin of the parent-child relationship. He becomes secondary.

Christ-Centered Life Demonstrated Through Family Living (Colossians 3:16-21)

Paul emphasized life in Christ in this section of Colossians. He climaxed his appeal in verse 16. He exhorted the believer, "Let the word of Christ dwell in you richly in all wisdom." He stressed the importance of having Christ at the center of one's life. Paul's primary illustration of the Christ-centered life is the context of the family. In verses 18-21, he applied Christ to the life of the family.

If a person is allowing Christ to dwell within him richly, he will exhibit Christ in the home. The relationships husbands and wives have together, the relationships that parents have with their children, and the relationships children have with parents directly reflect their walk with Christ.

Increasing Our Faith Through the Family (Hebrews 11)

Hebrews 11 records many examples of those who had faith. The list reveals that in most of these cases, faith was built in the context of the family. When faith became stronger, it was through the refinery of faith relationships. This indicates that if God is going to build faith, and if faith is being tested, it will more than likely occur in the home. There are 20 examples of faith listed in the chapter. Of these, 15 (75%) involve stories of family relationships. The following list reveals this:

Verse(s)	Name(s)	Family (numbered)	Faith Area
3	Christians	None explicit	Faith to accept God as Creator
4	Abel	Two brothers (1)	Faith despite others' failures
5	Enoch	None explicit	Pleased God and was translated
7	Noah	Family (2)	Saving of household
8-12	Abraham, Sarah	Husband, wife (3)	Faith to obey God and to bear child
17-19	Abraham, Issac	Father, son (4)	Faith to give child to God
20	Isaac	Father, Two sons (5)	Faith to bless children
21	Jacob	Grandfather, Grandsons (6)	Faith to bless grandchildren
22	Joseph	Son, Father, Grandfather (7)	Faith for godly heritage
23	Amram, Jochebed	Moses' parents (8)	Faith for son's safety

24-26	Moses	Family of origin (9)	Faith to follow family's faith
27	Moses	Son of Pharaoh	Faith despite wrath of Pharoah
30	Israelites	None explicit	Faith to conquer Jericho
31	Rahab	Family (10)	Faith for family's safety
32	Gideon	None explicit	Faith to follow God's directions and overcome Midianites
32	Barak	None explicit	Faith to respond to God's call through prophetess Deborah
32	Samson	Delilah, Parents (11)	Faith to fulfill calling
32	Jephthah	Son of Gilead, brothers (12)	Faith when rejected by family
32	David	Family (13)	Faith despite personal failure

| 32 | Samuel | Son, Mother (14) | Faith for complete dedication |

Pastoral Care for Families

Four Common Family Difficulties

Families encounter some common problems. One of these is *communication*. Families represent a network or system of relationships. This system requires effective communication. A breakdown or distortion in communication affects relationships.

Another common problem is *finances*. Finances represent the ability of a family to acquire, manage, and distribute resources. A dysfunction in one or all members of the family in this area affects the goods and services the family is able to receive and manage.

Emotions also contribute to the problems of a family. People talk with words, but their emotions communicate much more. Emotions become the glue for good or bad in family relationships. Sometimes that bond is so enmeshed that there is no flexibility, only dominance and manipulation.

A final problem area concerns *relationships* between parents and children. These problems range all the way from irresponsibility to abuse. What is intended by God to be a nurturing relationship sometimes turns out to be a selfish, nonnegotiable battle between family members.

Other family problem areas often are related to the four basic areas mentioned. These other areas can include difficulties with in-laws, adjustment to a stage in life development, moving to another area, extramarital affairs, teenage promiscuity, school difficulties, and child discipline.

Central Purpose of the Family and the Will of God

The family unit must seek the will of God together. The Lord has a direction for each person within the family. And God is involved in each relationship within the family system. However, the family as a whole must seek God for His will for them as an entire family. God has a message He desires to communicate through the family together. This was especially recorded in the Old Testament. In particular, the Book of Ruth illustrates this principle. The family of Ruth, Naomi, and Boaz received a message of God's mercy and care. God blessed the family and they continued. Their message did not die. In the same way, God desires to speak through family units today.

Gather Family History Information

A family's history is an important part of the counseling relationship. Many assumptions can be made about families in general. The pastor needs to find out what assumptions can reasonably be made about the particular family he is counseling. The best way to particularize information about a family is to search out the family history. The most effective way is to make information gathering a part of the counseling session. The pastor can then observe and respond to the way in which the family interprets its history.

The pastor can ask about significant parts of a family's history. Childhood relationships with parents are important. These relationships have formed significant behavior patterns. The behavior observed in a counseling session is due in large part to the way parent-child relationships developed. These include the relationships within the current family. It also includes the relationship the father had with his parents and the relationship the mother had with her parents.

When looking at parent-child relationships and their relationships with other families within the extended family, it is helpful to observe the way these relationships affected the identity and well-being of the family being counseled. These other relationships may have significantly shaped or altered the moral or spiritual nature of the family being counseled. The other relationships may have been adopted as models for relationships. Consciously or unconsciously, specific behaviors or opinions may have been adopted into the family. Knowledge of the impact these other families have had upon the family being counseled can be very helpful.

The family's history of involvement with the church is important. A family develops a relationship with the church they attend over the course of time. This relationship is usually related to significant events. Identification of these significant events, whether positive or negative, can be helpful. The critical feature to observe is the way in which these events were perceived. Understanding the way these events affected the family will provide not only historical information but spiritual insight as well.

Regarding spirituality within the family, it is especially helpful to understand the perception children have had of their parents' spiritual maturity. This includes the perception of children in the family currently being counseled. It also includes the perception the mother and father have of the spirituality of their mothers and fathers. These perceptions generally have a significant impact upon children. Whether positive or negative, the children had to respond. Their response was based upon their perception of their parents' spirituality. The important issue is not the actual spiritual condition of the parent as much as it is the child's perception of the parent's spirituality.

Much of this information can be gathered while simply recording a time line of the history of the family. Simply take a blank piece of paper, draw a single line down the middle, and ask the family about significant dates and events. As they discuss these, place dates and events on the time line in order. The notations may be brief. They need not be elaborate. The significance in the time line is not the actual record of events. Rather, the time line is important because it gives the pastor an accurate picture of this family's own unique history and the way the family views its history. This insight enables the pastor to deal more specifically with the family.

Discerning the Functioning of the Basic Family System

The family is a system of relationships. The individuals in the family do not exist apart from one another. By virtue of their biological or adopted origins, they are related to one another. No matter how good or bad these relationships are, the members of the family are in relationship to one another.

Within the larger relationship of the family are a number of smaller relationships. These include the relationship between mother and father, relationships between brothers and sisters, and relationships between parents and children. To some extent, they also include relationships with extended members of the family, such as grandparents, aunts, uncles, and cousins.

All these relationships may not function very well. Relationships may be distorted. They may even be abusive. Despite the level, intensity, or health of these relationships, they still function together. They affect one another and have some level of determination upon one another.

In the counseling process, the pastor must discern the nature and level of functioning between these relationships. Observation of the way in which parents relate to each other, children relate to one another, and parents and children relate to each other is important. Insight into these relationships when counseling families is as important as, if not more important than, seeing differences within individuals. Family problems stem from relational difficulties as much as, if not more than, from personal problems.

An effective way to record family functioning is to construct a family tree, or *genogram*, on a blank piece of paper. The genogram can be drawn while talking with the family. Individual members of the family can be symbolized with lines drawn to attach them. Other family members such as grandfathers and grandmothers can be identified. Birth dates, dates of deaths, and other significant information can be noted next to specific names. Issues can be identified and perspective gained while recording the genogram, and it can become a counseling tool.

Determine Whether the Problem Is Individual or Group in Nature

Problems can be centered in an individual or they can affect the entire family. A husband may be dealing with a personal issue, and its effect upon his wife or children may be minor. An example might be a theological issue or question. At other times, a person may have a problem that is affecting him greatly. An example would be a conflict at work. The husband brings the conflict home through carryovers in attitude and emotions. He may think it does not affect his family, but it does.

The pastor must discern whether a problem is more individual or family-related. The counseling concerns for individuals vary. If it is an individual issue, individual counseling may be more appropriate. If it is a family issue, family counseling is the most effective approach. In individual counseling, family issues may be related, and they can be addressed in the context of individual counseling. However, if it is actually a family issue, addressing it merely as an individual issue could be counterproductive. The whole family should be involved in the counseling and caring process.

Monitor Family Communication Skills

In observing the family, the pastor can carefully observe the way the family communicates with one another. The actual substance of the conversations and the emotional communication taking place are important. The emotional communication is especially insightful. Individuals not only say words, but they feel their words. These emotions in communications can be observed through verbal and nonverbal indicators. Verbal indicators include words, inflections, and voice pitch. Nonverbal indicators include gestures, posture, and distance. Observation of these indicators helps the pastor gain insight into the manner and level of communication between family members.

Often, in communicating and relating to one another, family members may make another member of the family a scapegoat. The scapegoat bore the sins of the community in the Old Testament. In similar fashion, family members may place blame, negative emotions, or pressure they feel upon another member of the family. Frequently, everyone in the family chooses the same scapegoat. For example,

Mom and Dad may feel bad toward one another about a financial problem. At the same time, they may feel afraid to show their negative emotions about one another. Both of them would then unload those negative emotions upon their son while talking to him about his school problems. This transfer of emotions is called scapegoating. They feel better because they are no longer carrying around those emotions. But the scapegoat feels the weight of what everyone else has dumped on him.

Assessment of the Family's Level of Coping

Families develop ways of dealing with stress. When a crisis or problem arises in the family, the family responds with certain ways of coping. These coping mechanisms develop over the course of time. They are passed on from family to family. Or they may be the result of some new influence upon the family. A family may develop a new way of coping in response to a new kind of problem.

Families learn to cope in a variety of ways. These ways may be positive or negative, godly or ungodly. The common thread is that families use them to adjust to problems and crises.

Some of the positive and godly ways of coping include times when the family responds by drawing closer to the Lord. They may seek the help of a friend or the pastor. The family may take a brief vacation or trip. They may have learned to sit down and work on the problem together. There may be an overall increase in devotion, prayer, and Bible study.

At other times, families may cope in negative or ungodly ways. The family members may isolate themselves from one another. Some families feel they cope best by yelling and screaming. Other families may isolate or scapegoat one particular member of the family. Sometimes abuse is used as a coping method.

Identification of the family's coping style assists the pastor in the counseling process. The pastor may then focus on replacing negative practices with new and better methods of coping. The good coping methods the family has should be reinforced. The absence of any coping methods creates a real crisis situation, and identification of this void could be used by the pastor for counseling. The pastor may simply give the family an assessment of what coping resources they do and do not have. This kind of awareness may be new for the family. It can give them insight about changes they need to make.

Suggested Methods for Ministering and Guiding Change in Families

The immediate concern of the pastor in family counseling is to get the entire family in for counseling. If it is indeed a problem that affects the whole family to a significant degree, the whole family needs to come for counseling. Some of the children may be older and have moved out of the home. If the issues do not currently involve them, they would not need to come to the counseling sessions. However, the family members who are being affected need to come. If a good amount of the focus is upon one or two relationships within the family, then a portion of the family can come to see the pastor. However, if the whole family is being affected, they all need to come. This is the first methodological step.

Methods of family counseling need to be directed toward specific goals. Family issues are very complex, but this does not mean that specific goals cannot be set. These goals may not address all of the problems. However, they will approach many of the critical issues. An important method is to write down these goals. This ensures that they are specific enough to be remembered. They become common for all the family. Write down goals and share them with the family.

Written exercises before, during, and after counseling can be helpful. One exercise could be the writing down of personal goals for the family. The family could also draw pictures and images of their family. Drawing a diagram of their family at work or play may be insightful. Before and after counsel, family members can be given scriptures to study. It may be helpful to ask the family to write down thoughts and issues that arise during the week. These can be brought to the pastor for his prayer and counsel. Writing and committing to a covenant can be a powerful tool.

The Minister's Family

The pastor must first address his own family. The pastor's family, like any other family, is not perfect. Not everyone in the pastor's family may be saved. The pastor's goal is not to have a perfect family. The pastor cannot make everyone in his family become a Christian. However, he can control the way he relates to his family. This is the first priority of the pastor's ministry to families in the church.

The way a pastor relates to his spouse and his family sets the tempo and paradigm for his ministry. The relationship style of the pastor is most critically tested in the home. He may appear one way to people in the parish, but he may act another way at home. The way he acts at home is a more significant barometer of his character than the way he acts in public.

Frequently, the pastor's family is placed under a lot of pressure. It is expected to be a perfect, flawless family. The pastor's children come under heavy condemnation when they do not act according to the perceptions and expectations of members in the church. This kind of pressure is unfortunate, unrealistic, and wrong.

However, despite the undue criticism made of the pastor's family by immature believers in the church, the pastor's family does serve as a witness to others. Even though the pastor's family is not perfect, it can still be in the process of growth in Christ. Though every family member may not be saved, the family can still bear a burden for the salvation of those that are lost. The pastor's family may not be able to share perfection, but they can communicate their care, love, and burden for one another. This can provide a strong witness of God's love and care working in a family.

Pastoral Care for Couples

Premarital Counseling and Care

Premarital counseling is an excellent opportunity for pastoral care and counseling. Even if there is some tragic circumstance such as premature pregnancy or sexual promiscuity, the very fact that the couple has now agreed to marriage indicates some reasonable degree of commitment. That commitment is an opportunity to minister. The couple is excited about the future and is willing to make significant changes in their lives. Pastoral counseling and care can guide and at times confront them about the nature and extent of their commitments in marriage.

This section of this chapter suggests a four-session model for premarital counseling, though there may be more or fewer sessions involved. However, the basic issues covered in this proposal could be adjusted to other time frames. The first session covers several issues: spiritual condition, problems from the couple's own perspective, and traits which make for godly marriages. The second session emphasizes the nature and impact of their individual family backgrounds. The third session deals with marital and family roles as defined in Scripture. The final session reviews the wedding ceremony, the honeymoon and wedding night, and the biblical basis of the couple's physical intimacy together.

Various emphases need to be made during the sessions. The biblical themes covered earlier in this chapter can be covered to communicate godly roles for marriage. The perspective of the couple is important because they have their own particular needs. The family issues each member of the couple brings to the marriage represents decades of development. Becoming one does not occur overnight. Working through their own past family histories and integrating their new life together is an important task. Physical intimacy must be addressed from a biblical perspective. The couple must take this opportunity to ask questions they may have little opportunity to ask in the future. They must be assured that this is a godly and fulfilling part of their life together.

The First Meeting With a
Married Couple for Counseling

The first meeting with a married couple is very important. Many times a couple does not return a second time. The pastor may have only the one meeting in which to deal with a problem. The couple usually has some apprehension concerning even one meeting. They may feel anxious about meeting beyond one time. Other problems may occur. Frequently, they feel satisfied after only one session and never arrange for another meeting. Though the pastor may feel the couple needs more counsel, the couple may not want to meet again.

During the first session there are some goals that deserve consideration. One goal is to hear the perspective of each of the partners. One partner should not dominate the whole perspective. The level of commitment between them should be enhanced. A significant goal is to help them feel an increase in their level of commitment by the time they finish seeing the pastor, even if only for one time. Another goal is assisting the couple in gaining insight into the nature of the problem they are dealing with. Still another goal is to give the couple specific direction about the issues they are dealing with. A final goal is to place the problems the couple is dealing with in the context of faith, equipping them to bring their problems to the Lord for His intervention.

The Wish Syndrome of Marriages

The problems couples encounter can be analogous to the process of grief and crisis discussed in chapter 9. In marital difficulties there has usually been a sense of loss. Romance, finances, feelings, stability, and trust may have been lost in the relationship. Marital counseling may be similar to counseling in the midst of the grief process. The couple can be guided in the emotional difficulties of the initial stage. They can be assisted in the heartfelt cry of the middle stage. They can also be led to recovery in the latter stage.

The wish syndrome of marriages occurs when one or both of the partners does not face the reality of the issues and losses they are experiencing. They wish that things were like they used to be. They wish that problems would go away. They wish that a particiular thing had never happened. The wish syndrome can be very damaging because very little effective change can occur as long as it persists.

The couple must have a basic admission and agreement about the problems and issues they are facing. This is a major undertaking in counseling couples. It means changing assumptions and attitudes. It changes the shape of their hopes about the marriage. However, unless the couple can agree on what their problems are and unless they can admit that those problems exist, resolution is very unlikely. At best, the couple will find some way to cope. The problem is that many times they find an unscriptural means of coping.

Issues to Identify in Marital Counseling and Care

Many of the issues covered earlier regarding families can be applied to couples. Time lines and genograms are necessary and effective. Issues of family systems of relationships, communication issues, and the relationship of the couple to the larger family are all important. The dynamics of family counseling can apply to couples counseling.

Additional issues need to be pursued in working with couples. The couple must deal with learning more effective ways to communicate with each other. Achieving more understanding of each other's perspective and experience is an important issue. Achieving a deeper sense of unity is significant. Gaining ability and insight into the emotional needs of each other is helpful. Other issues include flexibility, sensitivity, ability to revise hopes, and gaining skill in working out conflicts. The most significant issues for the couple revolve around spiritual priorities.

Two basic communication issues deal with spouses' ability to listen to the words and feelings of their partner and then communicate their words and feelings effectively. The problem arises when individuals begin seeing their partner only from their own biased perspective. Also, partners sometimes communicate caring only to unload what they are feeling without being sensitive to the feelings of the other.

A pastor can model care and listening. In the meetings he has with the couple, he can listen attentively and then encourage the couple to do the same, especially to each other. The pastor can place value upon what each of the spouses is saying. In turn, he can encourage the couple to place importance and value upon what the other partner is wanting to communicate. Unless a couple learns to communicate effectively, it will be difficult to address other issues.

Partners' understanding of each other and respect for each other is a very important issue. Frequently husbands and wives confuse the word *clone* with *couple*. Rather than a marriage partner or a mate, an individual acts as though he wants a clone of himself. The expectation is that there is only one way to see things, one way to act, and one way to respond—his way. This is a direct violation of God's creation of the uniqueness of an individual. It is a reflection of extreme self-centeredness.

A God-centered perspective understands and respects the uniqueness of others, especially one's mate. This does not negate right and wrong. However, the rightness or wrongness of something should be seen from God's perspective. Achieving that perspective will lead to mutual understanding under God. The alternative is a self-centered misunderstanding which attempts to make a clone of one's partner.

Unity in the partnership is an important issue. If the couple has children, they must show unity to the children. They must also show unity to their in-laws and others. This is not to endorse insincerity. It is not an encouragement to pretend a unity that does not exist. However, the couple must work out any disagreements in private, not before an audience. The couple must strive to achieve unity.

The ability to share hurts and be emotionally available to one another is important. Many times individuals feel that their partner does not care about or sincerely feel the weight of their hurts. As a result, they either do not share those hurts or they share them with others. Neglecting to share hurts with your spouse and sharing them only with others creates affection with others and avoids emotional affection with your mate. The pastor can be the one to facilitate the sharing of affections. He can encourage the couple to be open and available to hear each other's hurts.

A critical issue at the heart of marital difficulty is the spiritual condition of the couple. This area cannot be neglected. God is the key to the most effective change for a couple. If the couple's relationship to God is not clarified, then it will be difficult to determine how open they will be to the work of God in their lives. Salvation is a basic requirement for both partners. As the couple matures in genuine spirituality, their ability to grow and overcome issues increases.

Goals for Marital Counseling and Care

A number of overall goals must be kept in perspective when counseling and caring for couples. Much of the importance of these goals revolves around spiritual priorities. A central goal is placing first priority upon seeking and maintaining a recognition of God's presence and power in the life of the couple. In connection with this is the goal of being obedient to God's direction and commands to the couple. Another goal is understanding that their commitment to one another is a barometer of their commitment to the Lord.

Another goal is to apply their commitments to the Lord and each other into specific behaviors and changes in their relationship. Yet another goal is to develop new skills and abilities that make for an effective marriage. And a final goal is to learn to submit to one another in the fear of the Lord.

Summary

Scriptural paradigms are the foundation of becoming a shepherd. Contemporary models are important. However, Scripture remains the standard. Clarity about the paradigms from Scripture is important for pastor and church. Becoming a shepherd in today's world must be rooted in Scripture.

God–centeredness, being theocentric, is the root of the scriptural paradigm of shepherding. In Ezekiel 34 and in the New Testament pattern set forth by the Chief Shepherd (John 10), the summary of the pastoral task is to minister in such a way that the people of God will know that God is God. Knowing that He alone is God is to place Him at the center and origin of the church and ministry.

A working model has been presented. As mentioned in the acknowledgments section at the beginning of this book, the model has been implemented at Mount Olive Church of God in Cleveland, Tennessee, under the leadership of senior pastor Gary Sears. Any "ivory tower" concept was thrown out a long time ago in the process of the church's becoming God–centered, growing, and being blessed by God in many ways. Many other pastors and ministerial students have adopted God–centeredness as a paradigm for pastoral ministry.

What is God doing in your life and church? If you cannot answer that question, you have your first assignment. If you know the answer to that question, then you have the center and origin around which to minister and be the church.

Every aspect of becoming a shepherd—that is, the pastor as an individual (section 1 of this book), ministering to the body (section 2), and caring for individuals and families (section 3)—reaches into contemporary life because God is reaching into contemporary life. The church will never be antiquated, because it is not dependent upon you or me or a method. Scripture proclaims the church lives to know and declare that God is God, the center of all shepherding ministry.

BIBLIOGRAPHY

Adams, Jay Edward. *Shepherding God's Flock: A Preacher's Handbook on Pastoral Ministry, Counseling, and Leadership*. Grand Rapids: Baker Book House, 1979.

Anderson, Douglas A. *New Approaches to Family Pastoral Care*. Philadelphia: Fortress Press, 1930.

Anderson, James Desmond. *The Management of Ministry*. San Francisco: Harper & Row, 1978.

Arnold, William V. *Introduction to Pastoral Care*. Philadelphia: Westminster Press, 1982.

Bennett, George. *When They Ask for Bread*. Atlanta: John Knox Press, 1978.

Blackwood, Andrew W. *The Growing Minister, His Opportunities and Obstacles*. New York, Abingdon Press, 1960.

Bonhoeffer, Dietrich. *Spiritual Care*, translated, with an introduction, by Jay C. Rochelle. Philadelphia: Fortress Press, 1985.

Brandon, Owen. *The Pastor and His Ministry*. London: S.P.C.K., 1972.

Bratcher, Edward B. *The Walk–On–Water Syndrome: Dealing With Professional Hazards in the Ministry*. Waco, Texas: Word Books, 1984.

Browning, Don S. *Religious Ethics and Pastoral Care*. Philadelphia: Fortress Press, 1983.

Brueggemann, Walter. *The Prophetic Imagination*. Philadelphia: Fortress Press, 1978.

Bubna, Donald L. *Building People Through a Caring, Sharing Fellowship*. Wheaton, Ill.: Tyndale House Publishers, 1978.

Campbell, Alastair V. *Professionalism and Pastoral Care.* Philadelphia: Fortress Press, 1985.

_____. *Rediscovering Pastoral Care.* Philadelphia: Westminster Press, 1981.

Capps, Donald. *Pastoral Care: A Thematic Approach.* Philadelphia: Westminster Press, 1979.

Chambers, Oswald. *Workmen of God: The Cure of Souls.* London: Oswald Chambers Publications Association, 1965.

Corey, Stephen Jared. *The Preacher and His Missionary Message.* Nashville: Cokesbury Press, 1930.

Dale, Robert D. *Growing a Loving Church: A Pastor's Guide to Christian Caring.* Nashville: Convention Press, 1974.

_____. *Surviving Difficult Church Members.* Nashville: Abingdon Press, 1984.

Dewar, Lindsay. *A Manual of Pastoral Psychology.* London: P. Allen, 1932.

_____. *Psychology for Religious Workers.* New York: R. Long & R.R. Smith, Inc., 1932.

Dolloff, Eugene Dinsmore. *The Romance of Doorbells: A Guide to Effective Pastoral Calling.* Philadelphia: Judson Press, 1951.

Eakin, Mildred Olivia. *The Pastor and the Children.* New York: The Macmillan Company, 1947.

Ewald, Bonnie M., and Carolyn S. Roberts, "Contraceptive Behavior in College–Age Males Related to Fishbein Model." *Advances in Nursing Science*, April, 1985.

Fenhagen, James C. *Mutual Ministry: A New Vitality for the Local Church.* New York: Seabury Press, 1977.

Foote, Henry Wilder. *The Minister and His Parish: A Discussion of Problems in Church Administration.* New York: Macmillan, 1923.

Fowler, James W. *Faith Development and Pastoral Care.* Philadelphia: Fortress Press, 1987.

Fray, Harold R. *The Pain and Joy of Ministry.* Philadelphia: Pilgrim Press, 1972.

Gee, Donald. *The Ministry—Gifts of Christ.* Springfield, Mo.: Gospel Publishing House, 1930.

Glasse, James D. *Putting It Together in the Parish.* Nashville: Abingdon Press, 1972.

Grantham, Rudolph E. *Lay Shepherding: A Guide for Visiting the Sick, the Aged, the Troubled and the Bereaved.* Valley Forge, Pa.: Judson Press, 1980.

Hamill, James E. *Pastor to Pastor.* Springfield, Mo.: Gospel Publishing House, 1985.

Harmon, Nolan Bailey. *Ministerial Ethics and Etiquette.* New York: Abingdon–Cokesbury Press, 1950.

Hedley, George Percy. *The Minister Behind the Scenes.* New York: Macmillan, 1956.

Hiltner, Seward. *Ferment in the Ministry.* Nashville: Abingdon Press, 1969.

Hoehn, Richard A. *Up From Apathy: A Study of Moral Awareness and Social Involvement.* Nashville: Abingdon Press, 1983.

Hudnut, Robert K. *This People, This Parish.* Grand Rapids: Zondervan Publishing House, 1986.

Hulme, William Edward. *Pastors in Ministry: Guidelines for Seven Critical Issues.* Minneapolis: Augsburg Publishing House, 1985.

Iverson, Dick. *Team Ministry: Putting Together a Team That Makes Churches Grow.* Portland, Ore.: Bible Temple Publication, 1984.

Jackson, Gordon E. *Pastoral Care and Process Theology.* Lanham, Md.: University Press of America, 1981.

Jones, G. Curtis. *The Naked Shepherd: A Pastor Shares His Private Feelings About Living, Working, and Growing Together in the Church.* Waco, Texas: Word Books, 1979.

Kemper, Robert G. *Beginning a New Pastorate.* Nashville: Abingdon Press, 1978.

Luecke, David S. *Pastoral Administration: Integrating Ministry and Management in the Church.* Waco, Texas.: Word Books, 1986.

McIntosh, Jan F. *Pastoral Care and Pastoral Theology.* Philadelphia: Westminster Press, 1972.

McKenna, David L. *Renewing Our Ministry.* Waco, Texas.: Word Books, 1986.

Meloy, J. Reid. "Narcissistic Psychopathology and the Clergy." *Pastoral Psychology*, Fall 1986.

Mitchell, Kenneth R. *All Our Losses, All Our Griefs: Resources for Pastoral Care.* Philadelphia: Westminster Press, 1983.

Moore, John. *A New Testament Blueprint for the Church.* Chicago: Moody Press, 1985.

Mueller, Frederick Ferdinand. *Ethical Dilemmas of Ministers.* New York: C. Scribner's Sons, 1937.

Nayce, Gaylord B. *The Art of Pastoral Conversation.* Atlanta: John Knox Press, 1981.

Oates, Wayne Edward. *The Bible in Pastoral Care.* Grand Rapids: Baker Book House, 1971.

_____. *The Religious Care of the Psychiatric Patient.* Philadelphia: Westminster Press, 1978.

Oden, Thomas C. *Crisis Ministries.* New York: Crossroads, 1986.

_____. *Pastoral Theology: Essentials of Ministry.* San Francisco: Harper & Row, 1983.

Olsen, Charles M. *Cultivating Religious Growth Groups.* Philadelphia: Westminster Press, 1984.

Person, Peter P. *The Minister in Christian Education.* Grand Rapids: Baker Book House, 1960.

Segler, Franklin M. *A Theology of Church and Ministry.* Nashville: Broadman Press, 1960.

Slusser, Gerald H. *The Local Church in Transition: Theology, Education, and Ministry.* Philadelphia: Westminster Press, 1964.

Smith, Fred. *Learning to Lead: Bringing Out the Best in People.* Carol Stream, Ill.: *Christianity Today,* 1986.

Speckart, George, and Peter M. Bentler. "Application of Attitude–Behavior Models to Varied Content Domains." Academic *Psychology Bulletin,* April 1985.

Thornton, Martin. *Pastoral Theology: A Reorientation.* London: S.P.C.K., 1958.

Tillapaugh, Frank R. *The Church Unleashed.* Ventura, Calif.: Regal Books, 1982.

Turnbull, Ralph G. *A Minister's Obstacles.* Grand Rapids: Baker Book House, 1978.